L.I.F.E.
after the
STRUGGLE

Also By Shaneil "PJ" Yarbrough

Born a Statistic: *Living Rejected, Agreeing with God*

L.I.F.E. after the Struggle - Guided Journal

www.ShaneilPJYarbrough.com

SHANEIL "PJ" YARBROUGH

L.I.F.E.
after the
STRUGGLE

Living In Freedom Everywhere

Published by Truth Publications, LLC

L.I.F.E. after the Struggle
Copyright © 2021 by Shaneil "PJ" Yarbrough

All rights reserved. This book, and parts thereof, may not be reproduced in any form without written consent from the author.

Cover Design: Truth Publications, LLC
Cover Photographer: Kyra Dismuke Photography
Book Editor: James Bullock, Ph.D.

ISBN: 978-17366-11210
For booking and other information about the author, visit
www.ShaneilPJYarbrough.com

This book is gratefully dedicated to My Parents

Biological
Charley Roy Nichols (1949-2013)
Marsheill Finley

Adoptive
Mr. Andrew Curley
Mrs. Ernestine Curley (1940-2011)

Spiritual
Mr. Alphonso Montgomery
Mrs. Monique Montgomery

All of you are important and a part of who I am.

TABLE OF CONTENTS

	Acknowledgements	i
	Foreword	ix
	Introduction	xiii
	A Poem to Little Shaneil	xix
1	A Life Worth Living	1
2	After	19
3	Finding Freedom	37
4	Everywhere	49
5	Live Freely and Love Deeply	77
	Disclaimer	97
	Share Your Thoughts	99
	Notes	101

THE
ACKNOWLEDGMENTS

I have so many people to thank! However, these sentiments are brief compared to my heart's overflowing gratitude for each of you...

Larry D. Yarbrough, Sr., you are my husband of 21 years, my closet confidant, pastor of fifteen years, and partner in all things. Thank you for covering me in prayer daily, believing in me, and supporting me. On May 20, 2000, you cupped my chin in your hands (I will never forget) before God and man as we sealed our vows with a kiss. I appreciate you making a sincere effort every day to love me a little more. Throughout the struggles, you have never left my side. From our wonderfully simple talks filled with laughs to our majestic trips, you make being your "Mrs. America" worth it. You are a God-fearing role model for our sons and the protector of our family. You have wiped my tears, assured me I will not fail and cheered me on to success. Thank you for reading early drafts and being my proofreader, again! I look forward to many more beautiful days ahead. Babe, we've still got it! You love me well, I love doing LIFE with you, and I love you!

L.J. and Lance, my sons, you are my motivation. Mothering is hard work, but both of you have made it a much less daunting responsibility. L.J., my firstborn, thanks for saying, "Momma, you're the G.O.A.T.!" I may not be the "Greatest Of All Time," but my prayers are being answered as I watch you navigate life with honor, integrity, and hard work. Lance, I appreciate your random (and silly) expressions of love – whether it is a hug or when you turn the bed back when I am tired, you know how to fill your "Mah" with joy. My love for each of you is boundless, and I am a better woman, mother, and person because I have the pleasure of having you both in my world. My prayer is that you will continue to strengthen your sincere love for God as He grants you a LIFE beyond your wildest dreams. I love you more than words can adequately express!

Exodus 20:12 instructs us to honor our parents, and we will live a long LIFE on the earth. Though the book's dedication displays honor and love for all of my parents, I want to briefly speak of them individually. Thank you for bringing me into the world to the late Dad Charley Roy Nichols and Mom Marsheill Finley. It has not been easy coming to terms with my story but having the chance to know you both has made the process more bearable. I love you both. To my adoptive parents, Daddy Andrew and the late Mama Ernestine Curley, I feel incredibly fortunate that you chose us (my sisters and me). Your commitment to providing a family

Acknowledgments

that wasn't defined by being blood-related means more than you will ever know. I love you both. Daddy Alphonso and Mama Monique, it's safe to say the readers of this book should thank you. You told me there was more. I appreciate you loving me unconditionally and challenging me to go further and continue sharing. I am blessed to have you both as an earthly example of God's Heavenly love. Whether we are having a "Shut up, Shaneil" moment or laughing uncontrollably, the two of you are steady guidance. Your passionate love for me undoubtedly shines through and makes LIFE better. I love you both.

To my sisters, Latosha, LaTreace, and Ashley thank you for honoring and respecting the call on my LIFE. As I look back over our lives, I have no doubt that God has had His hand on each of us from the beginning. I am in great anticipation of Him continuing to unveil the fantastic things that He has in store for each of you. Nothing can break what we have, a bond established through birth and then re-enforced through adoption. We have the responsibility and privilege of loving each other to honor God's perfect plan. I love all three of you!

Jamie Benton-Davis, my B.F.F., you are my quiet strength. You love people with a fire that spreads far beyond where you can see. You are right; you are the "strong one."

And to that point, I appreciate you always showing grace under pressure. Because of you, I have a rare story to tell, having a genuine best friend for almost four decades. You have been by my side every step of the way. I cannot imagine LIFE without you. I love you, B.F.F.!

Changing Lives Ministries Church (C.L.M.), you are my bonus family. I did not choose you for myself, but you have been chosen for me. I am honored to serve alongside you. Your prayers and support are crucial to my surviving LIFE. Thanks for loving me – just the way I am. I love you all.

She is not expecting this, but I want to specifically thank J.P. (Jessica) Mobley, my "Switch," for your comments, "Amens," and for sharing your thoughts as I was writing. There are too many to name "on my list" of individuals I consider to be "my people." However, I pray that each of you knows who you are as I include this list of groups: family, Covenant family, friends, and colleagues. I pray for all of you daily and give thanks for being surrounded by the best! I am sending love and blessings to all of you and pray for you to have LIFE more abundantly.

Madam Mayor Veronica Smith-Creer, thank you for saying yes to writing the foreword. You had no idea what I would ask, but you welcomed me like always, with a smile and warm hug. As a woman in the public eye, I greatly admire your enthusiasm, passion, confidence, grit, and faith. Those qualities allow you to take LIFE by the reigns and ride through it with grace and power. I pray that you continue to shine bright like the "Sonshine" you are.

Dr. Jim Bullock, thank you for agreeing to edit my manuscript. You were very careful in how you approached the text. Thanks for showing great sensitivity to my intentions. I appreciate your holistic view and your genuine interest in the final product. Your thorough work included suggestions for improvement, constructive comments, and impressive feedback to produce a high-quality manuscript. Thank you for accepting the task and providing invaluable perspective.

I want to thank the late Kyra Dismuke of Kyra Dismuke Photography. It is too unfortunate she could not see the final cover design, which entails her awe-inspiring photography. I will never forget how she did careful research regarding my personal preferences before our photography session – the railroad tracks presented a concern. Nonetheless, somehow, Kyra always found a way to capture every important detail on camera. It was on a brutally cold afternoon. Her "sidekick" assistant and husband, "Mister" James, came along, ensuring a great experience with guaranteed laughs. From the beginning, her friendliness and quick-witted comments set the tone, kept us on track, and gave me the confidence I needed. Kyra was such a talented photographer, and we (my family and I) were always thrilled with the results of her work. In addition to that, she offered excellent services and did not hesitate to do whatever was necessary to make sure we were pleased. This time was no exception! I am thrilled and honored that *LIFE after the Struggle* is one more way to honor her memory.

Timothy Johnson, Brand Owner of Truth Publications, when our lives intersected through our C.L.M. ministry work, I never thought we would have an author/publisher relationship! Thank you for accepting me as your first author. You are a phenomenal publisher and an even better human being. You are the "Truth" and, frankly, the total package! From conception to publication, you offered keen insight, respectful warning, needed encouragement, and thought-provoking silence at all of the perfect times. Thank you for maintaining a standard of excellence from the point of our initial conversation. I was confident from the start. However, the services you provided far exceeded my expectations:

- **Design** (book cover design and interior formatting)
- **Support** (personal consult, phone/virtual check-ins)
- **Publishing** (copyrighting, digital proofs, securing professional editing and revising)
- **Marketing** (digital e-flyers, website and logo design, pre-sale guidance, and book mockups)

Acknowledgments

I cannot say enough about the brilliant graphic design for the book cover and website! None of this would have been possible without your keen skill set, willingness to take risks, and ongoing support. Finally, the priceless feedback from your beautiful wife, Shaquanna (How can I leave her out?), made a dramatic difference in this project. I am blessed to have a publisher who I know genuinely wants to glorify God by presenting readers with quality books.

Finally, to my readers – many of you have followed me through my author's journey. In a sense, you have witnessed the struggle. Some of you readers have been there from the beginning – you have joined me in my heartbreaks, changes, mistakes, and ever-evolving perspectives. I want to take a moment to express my gratitude. I would have never had the courage to share my personal stories and vulnerabilities if it wasn't for my community's intense love and support. Every purchase, "Like," comment, email, and second you spend reading my work is appreciated. You are the reason I write.

VERONICA SMITH-CREER
FOREWORD

I am blessed to be co-owner of our family-owned business with my husband. For many years in that role, I was afforded a great deal of flexibility. I had the opportunity to volunteer on several boards and work with diverse organizations in the community. Those opportunities became a two-fold blessing as I had the chance to make a difference and encounter many people.

Few people walk into your life like a breath of fresh air and shine a light on you that has the power to convict and comfort you at the same time. I can say that author, Shaneil "P.J." Yarbrough has achieved both. For years now, she and I have crossed paths in the community and during ministry-related events. It did not take long for us to realize that we have kindred spirits. So much so that we have never called each other by name or even friend, but always "sister."

I am the elder "sister," yet Shaneil has often been my teacher without realizing it. She ministers from her heart with a passion personified through the faithfulness of our Father! She bore her soul in her autobiography, *Born a Statistic* and allowed her readers, family, and friends to see the past that created the person we know today. Sharing her life experiences encouraged us immensely and confirmed this familiar scripture, Romans 8:28, "All things work together for those who love the Lord and are called according to His purpose."

In this book, Shaneil continues to provide inspiration, giving of herself to touch lives. Her authentic transparency is relatable and causes us to look at our experiences from a different perspective. I, for one, can attest to the fact that what the world may have suspected and even announced as our destiny has no bearing on what God has designed for us! As you know, struggles (tough times, unfortunate circumstances, and unexpected tragedies) are unavoidable. When they come, we may initially feel imprisoned by them. We may not be in a physical prison cell but unconsciously demonstrate a less-than-free-in-Christ type of life. If that is where you find yourself today, do not worry, you have a chance to have *L.I.F.E. after the Struggle!*

My personal struggles have included the pain of sciatica, a colon cancer diagnosis, the loss of my mother and younger sister, and the decision to run for the Mayor of El Dorado – all in the span of two years! Research says that sciatica was supposed to be constant pain. And sadly, that is the reality of many who suffer from this condition. Thankfully, sciatica could not keep me from walking into the destiny God granted me! I have no doubt that colon cancer was designed to kill me. Navigating through this life-changing disease, treatment, and countless tough days, I am a cancer survivor!

My mother and sister's death (so close together) were devastating and unimaginable losses, but God reminded me that their legacies can and do live on through me! With each blow, it would seem that these attacks on my physical body and the emotional heartache of losing my precious loved ones had the potential to destroy me. Instead, with God's grace and mercy, they became my motivation to preserve and pursue the Movement, which resulted in me being Mayor! In what I describe as "HERStory," I became the first female and black Mayor in the history of El Dorado, AR. This honor comes with both blatant and unspoken attacks from sources seen and unseen. There are many challenging moments in my days as I face and endure what few people would even fathom. Needless to say, none of these battles are easy, but through Christ each day, I acknowledge that I am more than a conqueror!

Each of my struggles has brought about new reasons to praise God and another testimony that I can freely share with others. Indeed, what He has done for me (and P.J.), He will do for you! I encourage you to read this book whether you are currently facing a challenge or coming out of one. The fact is that life can sometimes be problematic. This book will minister to you and prepare you to go from struggling to shouting! Get ready to begin *Living in Freedom Everywhere*!

Veronica Smith-Creer
Mayor, El Dorado, AR
Elected November 2018

THE
INTRODUCTION

Why do bad things happen to good people? I posed this question at the opening section of the last chapter in *Born a Statistic: Living Rejected, Agreeing with God*, my autobiography. Sharing a lifetime of personal struggles in my memoir was a God-given assignment. It had to be written, no matter the cost (I do not necessarily mean monetarily). Knowing that it was a directive from God does not mean I immediately responded. Nevertheless, over about a year, it became clear through several confirmation avenues that led to my humbled obedience. Though it was one of the most challenging tasks I ever have had, it was also rewarding. The initial goal was to glorify God by documenting my life, birth to 40 years. I also wanted to appreciate my family and friends for their steadfast support and leave a legacy for my children. Little did I know my testimony also would motivate others.

Many people have asked when Part 2 will be available. Frankly, I would have to live another 40 years for that to happen. This book is, however, a continuation of the story. The subtitle, *Living in Freedom Everywhere*, is derived from *L.I.F.E.* in the main title. When one is facing family conflict, illness, financial strain, or work-related problems, struggles in life are inevitable. Perhaps you are like me, you have come through many struggles, and you are beginning to believe in the idea of "happily ever after." But you might also be in the middle of a struggle. Either way, this book is for you. If you are reading it, your experiences likely have led you to it. Jeremiah 29:11 declares that God has a plan for our lives. No matter where you are, you are right on track.

The saying "other side of the tracks" often is used in a negative connotation. "Tracks" denote railroad tracks. When railroads were built, they initially were used as the primary mode of long-distance transportation. The tracks became significant fixtures through a town. In some cases, the steel rails quite literally caused a divide between the town's most prosperous and poor areas. Recently, I heard a news report on the violence in the 1921 Tulsa Race Massacre. Historians continue to uncover the destruction of the city's Greenwood District, better known as Black Wall Street. This area, north of the Frisco Railroad tracks, provides one of many examples of the division the phrase "other side of the tracks" implies, or perchance at least figuratively. As I write this book, my forty-third birthday is only a few swipes ahead on my calendar. I never want to forget that I am a girl from the "other side of the tracks."

Introduction

I grew up in Calion, Arkansas. Down through the middle of our small town lay a pair of rail lines that distinctly drew a community line. I went on the "other side of the tracks" only to babysit children (in white families), pay the water bill, patronize the community store, or visit the lake. All my relatives resided and worked on my side of the tracks. Though the distinct differences in the two sides of town weren't often mentioned, they were understood. It took me many years to acknowledge that some people think the "other side" is the wrong side of the tracks – the undesirable side of town. Reflecting on many of my life experiences, I quickly could agree. But because I have witnessed my life unfold and blossom into more than I could have imagined, I do not. Consequently, I am glad I came from the "other side." And like the Apostle Paul in Philippians 4:12, I know how to be abased, and I know how to abound. Despite all the struggles I've had, today I am a blessed woman, wife, mother, career woman, and follower of Christ. All glory, honor, and praise belong to God as I presently live in freedom notwithstanding on which side of the tracks I am. In fact, I spend most of my time on the side of tracks that once were too difficult to access. This reference is not about materialistic items or status. Instead, it refers to being healed and whole. God has immensely changed and shaped me through the twists and turns of my journey. The liberty of being transformed by His grace, mercy, and love is never too far from my thoughts.

On the book cover, I am sitting on the side of a set of rails thinking as I hold an old photograph of myself. In the photo, I am age four or five. This photo of "Little Shaneil" is the only one I have of myself from birth until that age. The first time I saw this photo, I was about ten years old. When I discovered it, it was taped to the front of my Adoption Summary. Seeing this image made me feel as though I had found a missing part of myself. I always have taken good care of the original, a mini-wallet photo, with the dimensions of 2.5" x 1.75". It is incredible how something so small can have such a significant impact. Some thirty years later, as I decided what I wanted to convey in this book's cover design, I knew I wanted to incorporate an enlarged version of my "baby" photo. The day of the photo shoot, I had a full-circle moment as I sat there on the railroad tracks with "Little Shaneil" in hand and heart. It brought me great joy to tell her, "We made it. We survived. We're living in freedom everywhere after the struggle." It has not escaped me that I may be still viewed as the girl from the "other side of the tracks." In fact, every opportunity to cross over the tracks, experience, and learn, my hope is always to come back and share with others.

Introduction

As you read this book, my prayer is that you will become fully aware that life has a way of leading you to what you've always deserved. Learning to appreciate where you have come from, where you are, and what it took to be there is key. The theme scripture for my personal ministry, Revealed Ministries, is "I consider our present sufferings (struggles) insignificant compared to the glory that will soon be *revealed* to us." Romans 8:18 (GWT). There is more to be revealed in your life. I want this book to help you realize, clarify, and fully celebrate two truths:

> 1. Life is full of struggles,
> – and yet –
> 2. Freedom is available.

Throughout, you will notice "L.I.F.E. Affirmations," which I use often. These are intended to lead you into the *L.I.F.E. after the Struggle* God has designed for you. Repeating affirmations can boost morale and increase confidence. These personal commitments are merely words speaking towards the change you want to see, but action is required.

Let's jump right in.

A POEM TO
Little Shaneil

You Were, Now I Am

You were abandoned. **I am** adopted.
You were in foster care. **I am** an advocate for foster care.
You were hurt. **I am** helpful.
You were violated. **I am** a survivor.
You were motherless. **I am** a mother.
You were expecting the worst. **I am** hopeful.
You were treated as an outsider. **I am** overwhelmingly accepting.
You were an average student. **I am** an educator.
You were trying to end your life. **I am** a life coach.
You were a victim of racial prejudice. **I am** a lover of all people.
You were sick – physically, mentally, and emotionally. **I am** healthy, healed, and happy.
You were enraged. **I am** an encourager.
You were depressed. **I am** Divinely inspired.
You were mentally unstable. **I am** a motivational speaker.
You were hiding your story. **I am** an author.

You were, now **I am.**

CHAPTER 1

A Life Worth Living

I can recall many Easter mornings when the hymn, "Because He Lives," rang out in my childhood church home. The lyrics are known all over the world.

> Because He lives, I can face tomorrow.
> Because He lives, all fear is gone.
> Because I know He holds the future,
> And life is worth the living
> Just because He lives!

This classic, written by Bill and Gloria Gaither[1], has a powerful story. The Gaithers discovered that they would be parents for the third time during the time that the United States was beginning the second decade of involvement in Vietnam. Prominent national leaders were being assassinated, and betrayals of national and personal trust were at an all-time high. Such headlines caused the couple to pause and ask themselves why they would bring a child into such turmoil. Holding their infant, they composed the lyrics,

> How sweet to hold a newborn baby,
> And feel the pride and joy he gives;
> But greater still, the calm assurance,
> This child can face uncertain days
> because He lives.

This gospel treasure, "Because He Lives," begins with realizing an empty grave and shifts to hope for uncertain days because of one monumental event, the resurrection of Jesus Christ.

In *Born a Statistic*, I shared candidly about hard times, past hurts, poor decisions, struggles with depression, and even suicide attempts. Through these situations, I could remember countless lessons and sermons ending with the minister's powerful description of Jesus's death, burial, and His being brought back to life. I even learned about this resurrection in the roughly 676 weeks of Sunday School, church services, Vacation Bible School (VBS), and Baptist Training Union (BTU) all between the ages of four and seventeen. However, the over-arching message of hope dimmed when life became challenging and the days were long. I often ponder how I allowed things to fall apart in different seasons of my life. For a long time, I even beat myself up about how much farther I could be if I made other choices. I could blame the Devil or be upset with God, but that would not be fair. Neither of them is responsible for what I decide. Keeping that truth in mind, I know that I was given access to an all-sufficient remedy early in my life but failed to apply it. I now have a great appreciation for what I missed for so many years!

About two years ago, my health care professional challenged me to be consistent in my day-to-practices to live a healthier life. She challenged me to stay in touch, get regular checkups, and consistently implement prescribed strategies and medications for six months. It was a sure sign of aging when I picked up so many prescription medications that I also purchased a weekly pill organizer. Like most things, in the beginning, I was motivated (primarily by feeling poorly). After three weeks of staying with the regimen, I felt amazing! My overall quality of life increased significantly. Life got busy, I no longer felt bad, and you know what happened, right? I didn't refill the weekly pillbox. Another couple of weeks passed quickly, and the pain and discomfort resurfaced. My well-being was almost worse than it initially was. How did I allow that relapse to happen? I became distracted and exchanged temporary satisfaction for a permanent solution. This example about my physical health has frequently happened in my spiritual journey.

In my foundational years, I was given a permanent solution that I decided to use on a short-term basis. Week after week, I was provided with structure for knowing God's word and given access to a relationship with His son, Christ, my Savior. Through all that time, how could I have forgotten the significance of such an influential occurrence – His great sacrifice on the cross? Sure, life has its ups and downs, peaks and valleys but it should not have made me feel apart from God so much so that I decided I would rather not even wake to see the next day. Knowledge of the risen Christ and application of this truth are starkly different. Believers and non-believers often boast of knowing Jesus was raised from the dead but have failed to experience the power of it! The thought of someone coming back from the dead is not easy to fathom. Nonetheless, like many other things that are difficult to imagine, the Bible speaks of numerous individuals being raised from the dead (listed in chronological order).

> **Knowledge of the risen Christ and application of this truth are starkly different.**

- ❖ Widow of Zarephath's Son (1 Kings 17:17-24)
- ❖ Shunammite Woman's Son (2 Kings 4:18-37)
- ❖ Israelite Man (2 Kings 13:20-21)
- ❖ Saints in Jerusalem (Matthew 27:50-54)
- ❖ Jesus Christ (Matthew 28:1-20; Mark 16:1-20; Luke 24:1-49; John 20:1-21:25)
- ❖ Widow of Nain's Son (Luke 7:11-17)
- ❖ Jairus' Daughter (Luke 8:49-56)
- ❖ Lazarus (John 11:1-44)
- ❖ Tabitha/Dorcas (Acts 9:36-42)
- ❖ Eutychus (Acts 20:7-12)

Though each of these instances was a miracle, one resurrection stands out among the rest. In all cases, except for one, each person lived again, but as human nature would have it, they also died. The power of the sacrifice of Jesus' death (and what makes it unlike any other) and resurrection is that He rose never to die again. He lives! Calvary's cross is not only where Christ died, but also where our victory was made complete. When believers genuinely identify with the cross, it can be the turning point in living the life God intended for us. As we personally accept the fullness of this life, we gain reconciliation with God, the forgiveness of trespasses, and victory over principalities and powers. Such experiences are a manifestation of "life and that more abundantly" (John 10:10). Because of the cross, we do not live alone; Christ lives within us.

All the people mentioned above were sinful humans. Jesus lived the perfect life that none of us ever could live, and He died the only death that could compensate for our sins. It is quite an eye-opener fully to understand Jesus took God's wrath so we never have to experience it. Jesus died so that we could have a life worth living.

Speaking of a life worth living, I have been asked the same question numerous times, "Did you ever think your life could be as good as it is now?" Frankly, the answer is "no." In fact, I did not feel deserving of a "good life." Because of formative experiences, I was carrying baggage that shaped my view of marriage. I expected my husband to tire of me and disengage from the relationship. My history was telling me that people do two things: hurt me and leave me. At different seasons, anxiety and fear led me to push him away. I thought if I resisted hard enough, he would walk away and later be glad that he did. We stood at the altar and recited "for better, for worse, for richer, for poorer, in sickness and in health," not knowing that we would live out every aspect of those sacred words. The first several years of our union revealed things about me that I had been able to mask with smiles and an upbeat personality. I believe both of us were surprised by the weight of the reality of our wedding vows. That said, I did not feel deserving of a husband who would diligently and consistently love, protect, and provide for me. Struggling through the horror of my trauma-filled beginning, low self-esteem, illnesses, and especially mental illness, I felt as if I were too much trouble and not worth his time. Now, for 21 years, my husband has been everything I needed him to be for wherever I was. He never wallowed in self-pity and negativity with me. He created a space that inspired me to be a better person. He stood by me, prayed fervently, and walked hand-in-hand with me while God gave me the strength to pick myself up, time and time again. Our marriage is stronger than it ever has been, because we have been strong, together, through it all!

> **It is quite an eye-opener fully to understand Jesus took God's wrath so we never have to experience it.**

An added bonus to the "good life" is being a mother. Initially, the thought of being a mother paralyzed me. From a young age, I have loved children. I babysat starting at the age of eleven, and I was obsessed with my nephews, so why was I so afraid I would not love my own? Lacking a solid mother-child experience, I felt unequipped. People kept saying, "Oh, your instincts will kick in – you'll do fine!" My heart and mind were saying differently. I had no idea that I would begin to calm down as soon as I saw my beautiful babies in my arms. I did not know how, but I knew I was willing to endure anything and do everything for those little people. It has not always been easy! Like the rest of the maternal animal kingdom (i.e., a mother dog knows to lick her pups clean), some of the how-to's of motherhood came naturally. Other things, like being emotionally available, made me question whether I could love my babies the way they deserved. But before I knew it, mothering indeed became second nature. Now? I cannot imagine my life without my two sons. Being their mother is both rewarding and fulfilling. Although my husband and I are authentically invested in preparing them for life, they have taught us valuable lessons in love, compassion, and humanity. Before being a mother, I had a plan and a very strategic checklist of how my life would unfold. I am forever grateful that my goals were trumped by what God had planned for me. I felt it was my job as a mother to make them better people – being a positive part of the world and making it a better place to live. And while that is true, the truth is, they have made me better.

    Finally, my church, career, and community involvement contribute significantly to my "good life." After tending to my first love, #My3Men, I happily pour time and energy into these areas because they matter to me. I find a great sense of joy as I help others. My life is happier because I remain active. For years, I had pessimistic thoughts and struggled to believe in myself enough to be involved. It took me a while to realize my strengths were born out of my weaknesses. As I engage in church, I have the chance to do a variety of ministry-related things. I have great confidence and comfort in this role, and I am grateful for having a small part in God's great work. While I am afforded many opportunities to be a speaker or play a leadership role in events, I have gratitude for serving above all things. Alongside my husband and Pastor, I am thrilled to share the joy of new parents, the pain of death, celebratory times, and offering prayer and counsel as often as it is needed. There is unpredictability about this work, but I am honored to be a channel through which the grace and love of God can reach others. My education career and community involvement constantly help me improve and allow me to give back. I use these acts of service advocating for causes I am personally passionate about – primarily women and children. I would never have guessed all the avenues that I have explored within these two areas. Not only is this part of the "good life" fun, but it also is satisfying. I have found that when I am seeking to be in God's will, I am the most joyful and fulfilled. The most rewarding part is helping others at the same time. All in all, I aspire to help others excel and take every chance to build compassion, confidence, and connection in each life that I touch.

The inquiries about my current "good life" arose mostly as I acquired the feedback from my memoir – the most personal form of writing. After people read my autobiography, both praise and yes, (a little) criticism flooded in. The most common theme was people's expression of gratitude for my so candidly sharing my personal experiences. I cherish the messages, letters, and emails that express the parallels people noticed to their own experiences found in the pages of my first book. The challenge of going to bed as a writer and waking up an author brought a weight to which I was not accustomed. It felt as if I had run a marathon. When I finished, I had a great sense of accomplishment! Finally, what had once seemed unattainable was complete. I was on cloud nine but unprepared for some of the reactions. Hearing feedback ranged from people telling me they loved or hated the book, it was life-changing or too transparent, too short or too long, and the list goes on and on. Writing my life story was the most vulnerable I have ever been. But I am glad that I finally wrote it. Digging deep was a way of honoring my soul.

It took me a while to be comfortable, knowing that I cannot please everyone. In our human nature, it's normal to want to go along with others. Yes, I hope to uplift, encourage, and inspire my readers, but I do not want to be controlled by their opinions and ideas. My main goal is to focus on pleasing God. The Apostle Paul spoke of pleasing God in three different passages: 2 Corinthians 5:9-10, Philippians 3:12-14, and 1 Thessalonians 4:1. These scriptures give me confidence as a writer and make the assignment to share what God gives me easier. When I realized (1) people would read what I wrote and (2) the readers would have expectations of me, I paused before transitioning into writing book two. Even so, I am excited to share the specifics of how life is better than I ever imagined! The only regret I have is that I did not enjoy a more satisfying life sooner. I have learned that situations can either define or destroy us. We can choose to learn from life's lessons or continue dealing with the same issues. When we align our lives with pleasing God (through His Word) and the incredible blessing of Jesus' death and resurrection,

> **When we align our lives with pleasing God (through His Word) and the incredible blessing of Jesus' death and resurrection, everything changes.**

everything changes. Regardless of what is happening in our lives, God and His Son make the difference.

Truly agreeing with God's Word and living in Christ brings a new perspective. The foundational scripture of the church I attend, Changing Lives Ministries Church, is 2 Corinthians 5:17. It states that if you are in Christ, you are a new creature – the old person has passed away. This passage informs us that as Christians, we are brand-new people. Nothing is the same. We are new from the inside out. It distinguishes the re-creation of an individual, which is much different from improvement or restoration. When my husband and I decided that we wanted to change our family room furniture, we started weighing our options. The table, chairs, and hutch were dated. We were on the lookout for something with a modern, new look. However, after we researched prices and compared durability, we chose to have our old items repurposed. The outcome was great! While we were pleased with our "do it yourself" (DIY) project, we were unwilling to pay the price to purchase brand new pieces. Thank goodness Jesus was willing to pay the price and go to the cross, and the cost had no bearing on our future. The precious gift of Calvary gave us a new identity in Jesus – we are everything He is. Because of that reality, infinite possibilities have been created for us.

A life in Christ is worth living when you understand the significant benefits. These advantages are plentiful. Therefore, I cannot mention them all. I would like to point to three of the benefits:

- ❖ Access to God
- ❖ Consistent and Constant Contact with God
- ❖ Godly wisdom

Access to God is at the top of the list because of the substantial role it plays. I have no shame in admitting that I have visited and often refer people to counselors, mentors, and life coaches. When I visit, my sessions usually are scheduled for a specific time frame with only limited access. We have direct access to God with no limitations. Secondly, through Christ, we have consistent and constant contact with God. We have the chance to talk to Him whenever and about whatever. Communication is a part of our relationship with God. God speaks to us, and we speak to Him. When Jesus died, there were no more limits, and we were no longer separated from God. The tearing of the veil (Matthew 27:51) represents that we are no longer separated from God. Through Christ, we have a personal connection to God. There is no more wondering what to do or whom to call when we find ourselves bombarded with deadlines, decisions, and dilemmas. By communing daily with God, I have discovered His wisdom is priceless. Godly wisdom gives us access to three things – the Holy Spirit's presence in us, examples of life's best practices in the Bible, and the opportunity to speak with God through prayer. Wisdom helps us to navigate life and make good choices. One of those choices is reflecting the character of God by loving others.

Finally, loving Him and our neighbor as ourselves (Matthew 22:37-40) are two of God's greatest commandments. This love, another invaluable asset, is exhibited through our service to others. Jesus set the standard of service with His sacrifice on the cross. Service to others is our purpose as Christians. We must put others above ourselves and be available to be the hands and feet of Christ; servanthood is our calling. One of my favorite rewards in this life with Christ is that God will use things for my benefit or the benefit of someone else, whether good or bad. "And we know that for those who love God all things work together for good, for those who are called according to his purpose," Romans 8:28. God has used every situation in my life to bless me, grow me up, further show His ability to do miracles or to be an encouragement for others. I challenge you to find the good in whatever state you find yourself in. I have no doubt God is putting things together for His glory. Knowing that whatever I experience will bring God glory provides me with the final benefit, peace.

A quote from Dr. Paul Chappell, president and founder of West Coast Baptist College, perfectly describes peace:

> Because of the empty tomb, we have peace. Because of His resurrection, we can have peace during even the most troubling of times because we know He is in control of all that happens in the world.[2]

Contrary to popular belief, Christians cannot avoid bad situations, but we can find peace amid them. It is a joy to have the great luxury of experiencing unexplainable peace that guards my heart and mind. Philippians 4:6 tells us how to obtain this peace: ". . .do not be anxious about anything, but in everything by prayer and supplication with thanksgiving, let your requests be made known to God." Even when I do not want to be disturbed or things are clearly uncertain, this peace is there to comfort me. I invite you to embrace the nuances of this often-quoted scripture. The

> **Christians cannot avoid bad situations, but we can find peace amid them.**

fullness of God's peace easily overshadows any concerns that may arise. I will elaborate more on the benefit of peace in Chapter 3.

In the face of never-ending highs and lows, we have what it takes to set us apart from those who have no hope, and we can share with those who do not know Jesus. God's plan, as referenced in Jeremiah 29:11, assures us that He knows our future and that His plans are good and full of hope. These major benefits are all a reality "Because He Lives": continuous access to God, His infinite wisdom to guide us, endless opportunities to serve others, the foundational belief that everything works for our good, and the unmatched peace of God. And because He lives, my life, your life, our lives are worth living.

> **The fullness of God's peace easily overshadows any concerns that may arise.**

L.I.F.E. *Affirmations*

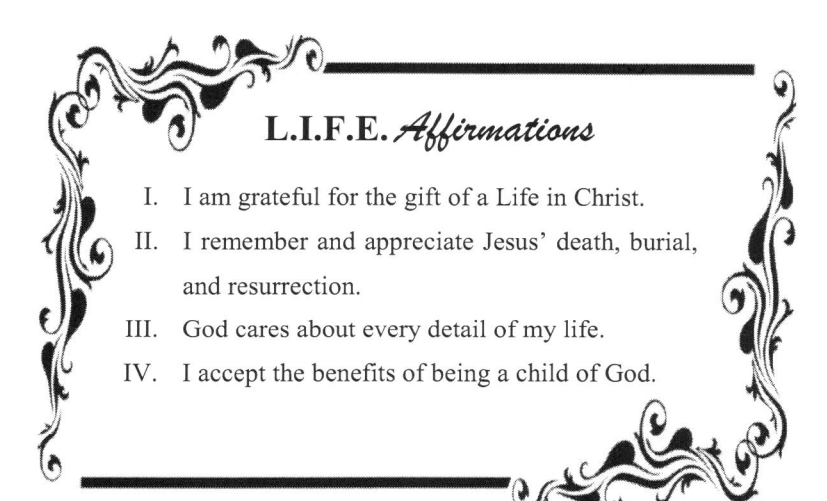

I. I am grateful for the gift of a Life in Christ.
II. I remember and appreciate Jesus' death, burial, and resurrection.
III. God cares about every detail of my life.
IV. I accept the benefits of being a child of God.

CHAPTER 2
After

"The events in our lives happen in a sequence in time. But in their significance to ourselves, they find their own order, the continuous thread of revelation."
- Eudora Welty, Author

The concept of a sequence of events pertains to several things in life. A sequence is defined as a particular order in which circumstances, movements, or things follow each other. Without sequencing, comprehension is less likely to occur. It is also an important part of problem-solving. Common practices such as reading a book, preparing items in the kitchen, following Global Positioning System (GPS) driving directions, and many other daily routines follow a sequence.

When I am searching for a good read, I begin by flipping to the table of contents to skim the chapters. After, I have a feel for the story's structure. There's nothing like a good book! Each morning, my routine involves a crucial sequencing of events. First, I make sure water is in the reservoir of my Keurig coffee maker. Once the water has heated, I place my cup under the spout. Then, I add a pod, and after, I enjoy freshly brewed coffee. Yes, coffee is essential! Think about the GPS. It is undoubtedly an appreciated convenience. I cannot remember the last time my family and I traveled a long distance before we checked for the series of turns to get to our destination. How did we ever live without it? Without the GPS offering the guidance of, "turn here, and then after, turn there" we literally would be lost.

Even when I was teaching young children, time-order words like "first," "then," and "after" were introduced to help in both literary and numerical lessons. Practicing beginning, middle, and ending sounds ensured phonetic awareness. Story maps and graphic organizers assisted students in identifying the parts of their writing assignments. The concept is easily integrated also into math, especially those dreaded word problems. And how can I forget science? Sequencing allows children to recognize patterns, predict outcomes, and understand how things work. I recall when my sons were toddlers, playing games to assess their ability to follow a sequence. I attempted to practice sequencing by narrating their actions: "First, put on your coat. Next, put on your hat. After, we will go to the car." It was always funny when they finished the first thing and then asked, "What do I do next, Momma?" Obviously, understanding that things happen in a specific order is crucial to success.

For years, I did not understand what was driving my need to know what will happen "after." I always have preferred alphabetical order and approach daily tasks with each step in mind. Determining the beginning, middle, and the after of a situation helps me move throughout life with ease. Even as a young child, I was sensitive to the sequencing of events. *Born a Statistic* reveals the many encounters with the sense of disorder that I experienced in my early years. With my being removed from my mother's care in what seemed like an abrupt occurrence, everything seemed to be in disarray.

In one foster home where I lived, overflowing closets in a dark room led to sleepless nights. In my young mind, I imagined those items to be scary, unidentified objects. Counseling later helped me realize that multiple instances of chaos fueled my cravings for stability in everyday life. Unsteadiness makes me so uncomfortable that I even find myself leery of surprises and nervous if a difficult conversation is needed, because I do not know what will happen afterward. As an early childhood educator with a great deal of research and training in child trauma, I can connect the dots between my earlier experiences and my responses to uncertain situations. Living through stress and frequent negative changes causes the brain to prepare for fight or flight. When this happens, the body has little time to recover and reset. Inadvertently, the body begins to react to future events based on the past. My husband and I have been married for twenty-one years, and he still has a difficult time pulling off a surprise. I have tried repeatedly to get used to being shocked, yet my immediate reaction is commonly unpleasant. Spiritually speaking, increasing in faith, that is, being sure of what you cannot see (Hebrews 11:1) also has been an ongoing journey in my Christian walk.

Like everyone, I have had my share of "first, then, and after" moments. I finally understand that if something happened, it is precisely what I needed, because God allowed all those things to happen. There are no coincidences in God. Life was not unfolding at the pace that I expected, and my reality was not what I had planned. I was stressed, anxious, uncomfortable, and annoyed. There was a season of my life when I thought it would have benefited me to eliminate the hard-to-deal-with portions of life. But now, I am confident that God was present in every step and consistent in each heartache. I find great joy in knowing that He held me yesterday, carries me through today, and has already secured my tomorrow.

Spiritually speaking, increasing in faith, that is, being sure of what you cannot see also has been an ongoing journey in my Christian walk.

While my beginning may have been ugly and the middle sometimes bad, I am finally in my "after" season, enjoying the good.

The Good, The Bad, The Ugly

My father has always loved watching western movies. When I was a child, I hated to see them coming on as I knew the T.V. would be monopolized for an extended amount of time. Westerns were not interesting to me, because they seemed dark, dusty, and delusive. As an adult, I have seen a few cowboy-themed films and enjoyed them. Perhaps the one I have heard referred to most often is the classic, "The Good, The Bad, and The Ugly." Full disclosure, I have never seen the film.

Nonetheless, frequently I have used the title as a phrase to describe my life. I decided to research the movie and its reviews to learn the plot. The story follows three men, Blondie "the Good," Angel Eyes "the Bad," and Tuco "the Ugly." The western conveys what the three endured to acquire some gold. The plot twist revealed that all of them knew the gold was located at a cemetery, but only Blondie, "the Good" played by Clint Eastwood, knew the exact location. One description I read said that the men had to put up with one another when all they wanted to do was kill one another. In the end, two of the men end up splitting the gold. To get the gold (much like an inheritance), they had to face hardship, trouble, and most importantly, stay in the race to the very end.

I can relate to this movie's theme on many levels. The only adjustment I might make is the order in which the title applies to my life. My experience has been The Bad, The Ugly, and The Good. With God's help, I did not let the bad deter me. Instead, I held on to the hope that there was an inheritance waiting for me! I will not give a full recap, but chapters one through four of *Born a Statistic* share the events that led up to my being placed in foster care. (Foster care itself and sometimes after adoption were bad) Time after time, I have been asked, "How did you get through all those bad times?" Penning my autobiography and disclosing that traumatic period's details allowed me to realize that my grief was turned into joy. This joy, no one can take away from me. Just as I am a mother who experienced the joy of birth, following the pain of labor, I realize first pain, then joy. The reality is that labor pains don't only come before a baby; they produce the baby. The child just comes behind the labor pains. But the baby is a result of the pain. The birthing joy I experienced both times yielded my children. They are two of the most valuable assets to my life. Therefore, I protect them and hold them close. The same is true for my God-given joy – it came through pain but is guarded and secure. Reflecting on the bad in my life allows me to see God amid tragedy. At one point, I thought the bad was insurmountable, but thankfully my story concludes with restoration.

From grade school, it was cruel to refer to someone as ugly. Ugly is considered repulsive, unpleasant, unsightly, or unattractive. Many fights were instigated with the insulting words, "You're ugly." Ugly manifested itself throughout my life in my poor choices, unfortunate circumstances, and ultimately a mental breakdown. If anyone had told me that all those things would eventually lead to blessings, I would not have believed them. The Bible says that we will be perfected through our suffering. 2 Timothy 2:12 even says if we suffer with Christ, we will reign with Him. This suffering comes in many forms and can be very ugly. With God's help, I did not allow the ugly to deter me. Much as in Acts 3:2, "And a man lame from birth was being carried, whom they laid daily at the gate of the temple called the Beautiful Gate to ask alms of those entering the temple," I was in an ugly situation but failed to realize that I was sitting at the gate, Beautiful.

Think of this gate, Beautiful, as the entryway to the good that the man was about to experience. The beggar was lying there lame, waiting on people to give him money, but he did not know he would be given much more. Peter and John were walking by on their way to the temple. Soon after they saw his need, they offered him the only proper remedy, Christ. Peter said, "Silver or gold I do not have, but what I do have, I give you. In the name of Jesus Christ of Nazareth, walk." The people that had known the beggar were astonished as he began running and leaping for joy. I can relate to the beggar, because things had been so ugly and bad that I could not imagine the good awaiting me. I am forever grateful that God sent people into my life who quickly assessed my need and offered me a newfound appreciation for fully accessing Christ. He has renewed my hope, restored my joy, dried my eyes, filled me with peace, and confirmed His grace in my life. Despite the ugly and the bad, honestly, I consider life to be so good now that I (and others) cannot fathom what it once was. That realization makes me think of one of my favorite Bible characters, Joseph.

The Joseph Parallel

As a young adult Christian, I struggled to make holy scriptures come to life and have meaning. My love for God's Word originated in Sunday School and Vacation Bible School as a child, but once those foundational days passed, I found a gap between the words and my experiences. I realized it was time for me to return to my roots. As I think back to those cherished days, I easily can remember my mother (Ernestine Curley), Aunt Katie Curley, Mrs. Hennie Long, and Mrs. Gladys Washington shaping my love for Bible stories. Their ability to help me identify story parallels was crucial. They always encouraged me to pray before reading and studying scriptures. Using that practice proved to be useful. Pausing to pray before beginning to study scripture adds light and truth. Sometimes I take a pause as I search and express my thanks for what I am learning. After my study sessions, to seal my reading of the Bible, I pray again. Finding parallels that will link the past to my present comes through this praying, studying, searching, and listening to God's Spirit.

> **He has renewed my hope, restored my joy, dried my eyes, filled me with peace, and confirmed His grace in my life.**

I have discovered what I like to call the "Concept of After" in numerous Bible stories. A few of my favorite *After* stories are below.

- Abraham displayed profound faith and obedience as he was willing to sacrifice his beloved son, Isaac. "After" he had tied up Isaac, God provided the ram in the bush. (Genesis 22:1-18)

- Joshua followed God's unusual instructions for the battle of Jericho. "After" Joshua's army marched around the city once a day for six days and seven times the seventh day, the walls came down! (Joshua 6)
- Esther, a Jewish orphan, bravely raised her voice and used her platform. "After" she stood up, Haman was exposed, and the Jews were saved. (Esther 4:14, Esther 7:1-6, 9-10 and Esther 8:1-8, 11, 17)
- "After" Paul and Silas praised and prayed in jail, an earthquake shook the prison, their shackles fell off, and they were freed. (Acts 16:25-34)

By far, one of my favorites is the remarkable display of the *Concept of After* is in the story of Joseph. For the sake of history, Joseph is the great-great-grandson of Abraham. His father, Jacob, is known for stealing his twin brother

Pausing to pray before beginning to study scripture adds light and truth.

Esau's birthright. Esau (Joseph's uncle) forgave Jacob for this deception. That detail is important, because that unlikely gesture is something that Joseph chooses to mimic later in life. His story spans from Genesis 37 to Genesis 50. It is easy to see that he is a special young man from his introduction as a seventeen-year-old. Joseph is described as talented and handsome. He was well-behaved and, frankly, his father's favorite. The latter would bring him many problems, because Joseph was the second to the youngest of twelve brothers. Jacob gave Joseph a "coat of many colors," which brought out his brothers' envious ways. As Joseph began to share his literal dreams with the family, his problems became even more significant. It was clear to him that God had specific plans for him. But the ideas of his destiny to be exalted over his brothers were not embraced. They hated him more.

Joseph's suffering started in his teen years. In his immaturity, he made the mistake of thinking that his family would celebrate his dreams. His brothers devised a plan to kill him. Their jealousy made them plot to see the downfall of Joseph. Initially, they threw him in a pit and left him there to die. Then to make sure Joseph would no longer be a problem, they sold him to the Ishmaelites. They dipped his coat in blood and told their father, Jacob, that they had found it. Jacob had over 20 years of mourning, and the brothers managed to keep their secret.

They forgot all about Joseph. As a slave in Egypt, a foreign land, Joseph would not forget as quickly.

I am hitting only the highlights. Trust me, the story is worth rereading. Even as a slave, Joseph rose to distinction. He found favor with Potiphar, Pharaoh's top official. Joseph was so trusted that Potiphar entrusted him with watching the palace in his absence. To his surprise, he also caught the attention of his boss's wife. When he refused her sexual advancements, he was done another great injustice and was falsely accused. Her lies led to Joseph's being put in prison! He had dealt with rejection and abuse from his brothers, was separated from his loving father, was sold as a slave, and now faced imprisonment for a crime he did not commit. To that point, stay tuned! In chapter three, we will uncover the innocent being imprisoned for crimes that they did not commit. What else could possibly happen to this gifted, God-fearing young man?

In prison, Joseph befriended two of Pharaoh's servants, the cupbearer and the chief baker. He continued to use his gift of interpreting dreams. Joseph told the cupbearer that his dream showed him being released. Joseph asked only that the servant remember him before Pharaoh. But the Bible says in Genesis 40:23, "he did not remember Joseph; he forgot him." To add to his list of struggles, Joseph was betrayed by a friend. He had every reason to be bitter, but instead, he stayed focused on what he believed was God's will and purpose. Joseph's responses to all his painful circumstances made the difference. No matter his suffering in the pit, at the palace, and in the prison, Joseph displayed honor to God in the "after." His release from prison and being rehired into Pharaoh's government set him on a path that proved just how much of a parallel he is to our Savior, Jesus.

It may seem small to some, but even the significance of what Joseph chose to name his children gives insight into his attitude. The meaning of his firstborn, Manasseh, is "It is because God has made me forget all my trouble and all my father's household." The second son's name, Ephraim, meant, "It is because God has made me fruitful in the land of my suffering."[3] Only God's work removed his past pain and pushed Joseph to speak these blessings over his seeds. I have heard it said that if we cannot get healed for ourselves, we should do it for our children. Joseph did not allow any bitterness from his past to access into his "after." Furthermore, Joseph was promoted to second-in-command of Egypt and was given charge of getting ready for a famine.

The widespread famine meant Joseph's brothers would come to Egypt to purchase corn. Immediately, Joseph recognized his brothers and could have had them punished or turned away. He did not reveal himself. In fact, the Bible says that Joseph stepped away to weep as he was overcome with the emotion of seeing them again. He was a godly man, but he was also human. After testing his brother's trustworthiness and seeing his younger brother, Benjamin, he knew it was time to reveal himself. This unveiling came with an outburst of Joseph weeping again, loudly, and as described in Genesis 45:1, 2, intensely. I can only imagine how the years of pain and struggles came gushing out of him in a flood of tears. Because of this release, he invited his brothers close and had a beautiful moment of truth with them. Paraphrased, he said, *This was all part of God's plan for us*. He did not rebuke his brothers. Joseph did not give them a lecture about all he had been through. He did not curse his brothers; he blessed them! Because Joseph allowed God to heal his pain, he was able to leave a spiritual legacy and impact many generations.

Thirty years passed between Joseph's first being sold into slavery and his family's reunion. Thanks to his humility, the family experienced full restoration. In chapter 50, verse 20, the "after" of the Joseph parallel can be summed up with these words: "You meant evil against me, but God used it for good." In my life and yours, things have come against us that were not pleasant. Those things had the potential to destroy us, but God can use them for our good! As we allow God to orchestrate the sequence of events that He has planned for us, the good, the bad, and the ugly will lead us to the "after" that is specially designed for us.

L.I.F.E. *Affirmations*

I. Through the highs and lows, I trust completely God's sequence of events.

II. I appreciate the good, the bad, and the ugly as possibilities for God to be glorified in my life.

III. [Like Joseph] I will have the correct response to wrongful treatment.

IV. I will enjoy my "after."

CHAPTER 3
Finding Freedom

I have a personal interest in incarceration. I know it is odd, but it is true. My interest in incarceration began in my teen years. Once I realized my biological mother had been jailed and imprisoned numerous times, I became intrigued with the prison system. I started reading books and watching TV shows and documentaries like *Lockup*, *Jail*, and *Women Behind Bars*. After watching, I would be haunted by nightmares and insomnia. I found myself contemplating the "arrest, release, and repeat" concept and began to do research. This concept essentially describes individuals with multiple arrests and their being released – only to repeat the cycle. All the while, I was fearful of even the thought of experiencing jail life. When my local leadership class participation included a local jail tour, I was terrified and excited! I still can recall the details of the building and the dark, gloomy atmosphere. My weird obsession gave me the nudge casually to mention to a classmate that while some inmates claim to be innocent, most are upfront about their wrongdoings and have accepted their consequences. She was really fascinated when I told her about a nationally known organization whose purpose was to help people serving time for crimes for which they were falsely accused.

Forty-six years is how long Richard Phillips spent in prison – for a murder he did not commit. To date, he has served the longest known wrongful prison sentence in America's history. Richard Phillips and many others have been failed by the entire justice system, and the Innocence Project works tirelessly to help such people. The Innocence Project, founded in 1992, is one that helps people to rebuild their lives. Their mission is to "…free the staggering number of innocent people who remain incarcerated and to bring reform to the system responsible for their unjust imprisonment."[4] Their work focuses explicitly on vindication through DNA testing of those wrongfully accused. The project's work has led to nearly 400 individuals' release from prison. Because the Innocence Project works to improve case law, reform policies, support exonerees, and lead education through science and research, the wrongfully accused go free. In 2019 alone, the National Registry of Exonerations (NRE) recorded 143 individuals as exonerees. Nearly 60% of these cases resulted from the work of the Innocence Project or related efforts. Based on their research, 17 of the former prisoners were freed based on DNA evidence or with the help of DNA findings.

Instead of going too deeply into the statistics, I will get straight to sharing an epiphany I had. There is a distinct parallel between the Innocence Project and God's ultimate sacrifice, giving His Son, Jesus Christ, for us to be free. Throughout this chapter, I will share three excerpts that follow the path of the beneficiaries of the Innocence Project.

> **To be freed, one must, at one point, been bound or imprisoned.**

It is easy to become engrossed in their stories, because there are uncanny similarities to their experiences and life before accepting Christ's gift bore on the tree (I Peter 2:24). The victorious statement from John 8:36, "So if the Son sets you free, you will be free indeed," serves as a constant reminder that in Christ, we are free. In Greek, the word *free* can mean to liberate or exempt from liability. To be freed, one must, at one point, been bound or imprisoned. As sinners, that is what we were – under the bondage of sin. In that same passage, Jesus mentions being a slave to sin. Before we knew

Christ, our sinful nature took authority, held us captive, and became our Master. We may not have been physically behind bars, but we were not in control.

Freedom Excerpt 1: Who's in Control?

I went to prison when I was 35. By that time, I had lived a full life on my own since I was 14. No one told me what to do. Being jarred by a bright flashlight at 5:00 a.m. to shower, clean up, and make my bed before the first inmate count of the day made me feel like I was a child. One C.O. (Correctional Officer) thought he needed to remind me that I had to do it his way, in his time. I felt humiliated. Most times, I skipped breakfast [next on the schedule] when he was working. I didn't eat because I wanted to show him... I was in control, not him! But my stomach proved to be the winner every time. Those days, I stood tall, waiting to be counted so that I could be released to eat lunch.

This inmate's aim was to have some sense of control. However, no matter what we tell ourselves, we do not have the power when held captive. In the above instance, the individual refused a meal to show the correctional officer who was boss. But the desire for self-mastery did not prove to be effective. Thinking we are in control and having control are two different things. When we are born again and accept Christ, we get a new Master. After God gives us a new nature and a new mind, He also fills us with the Holy Spirit. The scripture, II Corinthians 3:17, puts it in this manner, "The Lord is a Spirit, and where the Spirit of the Lord is, there is liberty (freedom)." We are free from our sins and the penalty of sin. With Jesus, the death sentence, the wage of sin mentioned in Romans 6:23, was revoked!

This revocation has afforded us both eternal life and unconditional love. The mind shift that is necessary to accept those gifts can be difficult. Satan, called the "accuser of the brethren," in Revelation 12:10, has deceived us into thinking we are not recipients of everlasting life and absolute love from God.

> **Thinking we are in control and having control are two different things.**

Why else do we experience feelings of guilt? How can we get over the shame of what we have done in our past? When will we finally feel as if God has really forgiven us and stop repenting again and again? We cannot be ignorant of Satan's devices. He is a liar, and his charges are false. The devil has no right to accuse us, because everything has been covered by Jesus's blood on the cross. Satan does not want us to live in freedom. He wants us to think we have not changed. Experiencing complete freedom requires the mind to be transformed.

Romans 12:2 provides the antidote for breaking free from conforming to the world and transforming from the inside out. The human mind is complex and can do many things. Funny enough, that is partly the issue. The mind is the storehouse of all knowledge and the tool we use the most. The mind is housed in the sophisticated organism, the brain. It is responsible for displaying thoughts, awareness, emotion, willpower, memory, and imagination.

> **Experiencing complete freedom requires the mind to be transformed.**

The problem with the mind is that it can become so bent on what it has seen, heard, and experienced that it has trouble accepting what it has not seen – God and His absolute supremacy. This is a trick of our great enemy. Satan does not want us to see God for who He is, "The god of this world [Satan] has blinded their minds to keep them from seeing the light of the gospel of the glory of Christ" (II Corinthians 4:4). He is bound forever and is terribly jealous of our freedom. Therefore, he plagues our minds with thoughts from our past, such as guilt, shame, and despair. One of Satan's biggest weapons is convincing us to look back on our shameful moments. If we do fall for this trap, we lose the chance to live and develop.

Finding Freedom

Freedom Excerpt 2: Outside but Inside

Twenty-seven years on the inside, I planned what I would do when I was on the outside. The people of the Innocence Project made that possible.

Up until I walked out, I didn't believe it. When they gave me street clothes and my belongings, my grandfather's watch was the first thing I looked for. I had been in prison so long, but I still remembered how the engravement, "There's always time." felt on the back of it. Grandfather was in Heaven, but his words would be my motivation to start again…I thought. I was glad to be outside, but it was a culture shock. Everything was fast. Too fast. It was too much. At the halfway house, I sit inside my room, eat my meals, and go back. Sometimes I go to the backyard and walk in the grass. That feels familiar – like I'm "walkin' the yard," it feels right – like the inside.

After receiving Christ, we are free, but we will fail to realize it unless our minds are transformed. As free individuals, we must act like it. We are free of the past, pain, and people's opinions. We must accept the grace that has been extended and not succumb to the weight of Satan's deception. Though we are not perfect, we are no longer imprisoned and can walk in the abundance of God's blessings and victory.

The final connection I would like to highlight with the Innocence Project is that their work evolves around deoxyribonucleic acid (DNA). DNA is the information storage system of most organisms, humans, animals, plants, and some viruses. It is where genes are organized and lead to observable traits. The project uses DNA testing to prove the innocence of their clients. In their years of research, it has been determined that 99.9% of human DNA is identical, but the remaining 0.1% can be used to distinguish one person from another. Countless individuals have been exonerated from charges that otherwise would have resulted in life in prison or a death sentence. The larger of the two numbers is 99.9%. However, it is not the most significant. Though small, it is the 0.1% that eliminates all uncertainty in these cases.

> **As free individuals, we must act like it.**

Several years ago, I had an ectopic pregnancy. My doctor's words, "You're the 0.1%," really stuck with me. As he explained that few women experience getting pregnant in their tubes, I saw the 0.1% as a curse. I desired to be the 99.9% and have the opportunity one day to meet my baby. His explanation made the 99.9% seem more favorable, but I had to view the situation from the spiritual aspect, not in my human nature. As humans, we are in many ways the same.

Finding Freedom

The late and great Maya Angelou said, these simple but no less powerful words:

> I am aware that I am a child of God…but I have to know that the brute, the bigot, and the batterer are also children of God, whether they know it or not. I am a human being, and nothing can be alien to me. If we can internalize that, we will never be able to say I couldn't do that….because if a human being did it, we have all the components that he or she had to do the same.

People see me in various roles – the woman, wife, mother, daughter, sister, friend, Pastor's wife, author, minister, colleague, life coach, educator, mentor, community volunteer, and motivational speaker – but a human is who I am, really. Yet, I am who I am because I belong to God through Christ. It has taken time, but as I have become fully established in following Jesus and finding my identity in Him, I have a new-found sense of freedom. Jesus' blood came to renew our minds, hearts, and our very being. The 0.1% of having Christ and His Spirit present in our

> **People see me in various roles … but a human is who I am, really.**

lives provides us with everything we need. This liberation has given me a renewed sense of purpose, commitment to helping others, and a passion for living life to the fullest.

Freedom Excerpt 3: The Rest of My Life

"In the years since I've been out, I decided I could spend the rest of my life being bitter, or spend it being a testament to God's blessings."
An Exoneree

In *Born a Statistic*, I introduced the idea of our taking the stance to *Agree with God*. Sometimes life throws you a curveball. And other times, you are hit by the pitch. It's easy to fall into thoughts like, "Where are you, God?" Sometimes it seems as if He is hiding. I'm not too spiritual to admit it – that there are times He seems absent. We know better, but we still have the pain, the tears, and hurt. But this is not the time to run from Him; it's the time to run to Him. Don't fall prey to the circumstances. Stay steady in the Creator, knowing that He is in control of our affairs. He has made us free. We are innocent because we have His DNA.

L.I.F.E. *Affirmations*

I. I choose freedom and declare that I am innocent.
II. Through Christ, I have conquered sin and death.
III. I am a new person with Christ's DNA.
IV. I have no fear, worry, insecurity, shame, or self-hatred.

CHAPTER 4

Everywhere

A well-known 1920's gospel song meant for children goes, "This little light of mine, I'm gonna let it shine. Oh, this little light of mine, I'm gonna let it shine." During the Civil Rights Movement, this song became increasingly popular and is tied to activist Fannie Lou Hammer. She sang this song while being detained by the police after attempting to register to vote.[5] The song lyrics are repetitive and straightforward and have the common goal of bringing people together for the common causes of unity and freedom. This beloved tune is easily recognized across the world, especially in the Christian faith.

Many believe the song is derived from Jesus' remarks found in Matthew 5:14-16 (KJV),

> Ye are the light of the world. A city that is set on an hill cannot be hid. Neither do men light a candle, and put it under a bushel, but on a candlestick; and it giveth light unto all that are in the house. Let your light so shine before men, that they may see your good works, and glorify your Father which is in heaven.

Also, in John 8:12, Jesus says, "I am the light of the world." Apart from Jesus, we live in darkness. Jesus, the Light, permeates into our lives, every crack and crevice, and brightens our very being. I found the reference of this light in the church pew's ruby red National Baptist Hymnal through the song, "This Little Light of Mine." I loved singing this melody as a young child, and I still love it to this day! One of the verses talks about the location of sharing this light by declaring, "Everywhere I go, I'm gonna let it shine. Everywhere I go, I'm gonna let it shine."

It sounds easy, doesn't it? Jesus is the light, and He lives inside me. Therefore, my light shining everywhere should come second nature. I wish I could say that this result of having Jesus inside me always has been manifested in my life, but it has not. I have known that the light has been within me for years. Having the light [Jesus] and allowing Him to shine through you is very different. For years, I was doing precisely what the Word of God said not to do – hiding the light. "Living Rejected" is a chapter (and a part of the title) in my first book. In that text, I talk about how I somehow convinced myself that no one wanted to be reminded continually about this light. At the time, I did not have a full appreciation for the latter part of Matthew 5:16, "…and glorify your Father which is in heaven." The light that illuminates in me and through me is for God's glory. While I struggled to be myself because of fear of not being accepted, He was robbed of what belongs to Him: all the glory! I found that these feelings of being uncomfortable and fearful were paralyzing literally everywhere. Whether at home, work, in the church and community, or with my family members, growing to the point that I could share my light everywhere has been a journey.

> **The light that illuminates in me and through me is for God's glory.**

Home

Recently, I purchased a customized wooden sign to hang on our front porch. The sign reads, "Our Happy Place." We strive to have a home of peace and tranquility. Our hope is that all who enter feel the warmth of the light that resides there and are free to be themselves. Several of our guests have commented about our house as a place for a good nap. I can attest to that for sure! Creating this environment has been intentional. Nearly 21 years ago, my husband and I happily moved into our first house located at 701 Gladys Street. Our first address was a four-room house. I believe my husband's favorite story to tell is that when the wind blew outside, the curtains would rise on the inside. It was not much to the eye, but it was ours! Soon after moving, we were eager to invite a couple of friends over. They were still living on the college campus and gladly accepted our invitation. Moments after arriving, one of them began making negative comments: "I don't think this neighborhood is safe, this house is tiny, where did this furniture come from?" Our feelings not only were hurt, but we were also angry! She was not invited again. After talking about the occurrence for a few days, we decided that anyone who visited would have to adjust to us, not the other way around. We decided we wanted our home always to be an uplifting atmosphere.

A few days later, we grabbed a sticky notepad and pen and started writing positive scriptures, words, and phrases. The notes were posted all over the house. From the front door to the bathroom mirror, messages were visibly displayed for our guests and us. Creating the home environment that we wanted to live in was necessary. Our families of origin were not the same, but we agreed that we wanted a peaceful, loving household. This strategy lasted for a while and provided us with a foundation for the years to come. In year two, we moved to another city as we started new jobs and were about to be first-time parents. The accumulating responsibilities and excitement of these times took first place. Therefore, our approaches to setting the tone in our new home were not as focused. By the time we became parents and our son was six months old, reality set in and affected our entire lives.

My autobiography, "Born a Statistic," gives a detailed description of how it became more difficult for me to be both present and emotionally available. Navigating motherhood, life, work, and social circles became doubly hard. I struggled with anxiety. When the prevalent postpartum depression set in, I buckled under the pressure. This depression led to my being detached from my family and hospitalized. My self-esteem, confidence, emotional intelligence, and communication were all lost during this time. When I returned home, I felt damaged, unbalanced, and overall broken. Being a wife and mother were my most valuable vocations, but I could not muster the strength to function in these roles. My home, which once had been my "safe place," where I desired to be free from negativity, transformed into a cesspool of hopelessness. I felt terrified, helpless, and alone. In fact, there were times when being outside my home was more comfortable than being in my personal space.

The people who live with you (my husband, in my case) know you better than anyone else. You may be able to fool the people you encounter for brief moments throughout the day, but those you reside with know the real you. My husband brought it to my attention that I was happy at work, church, and with friends but not when we were home. The impact of my inconsistencies led to arguments and my secluding myself – I was a prisoner in my own home. I desperately wanted to be free. This true freedom came through both spiritual and professional techniques. Years of this vicious cycle came to an end once I recommitted myself to starting my day with prayer and Bible study. Communing with God and reading His word gave me courage and assurance of His love. I realized God is not a bully standing over us with the key to our shackles in His hand. His Son, Jesus Christ, is the key to our freedom!

> **You may be able to fool the people you encounter for brief moments throughout the day, but those you reside with know the real you.**

With a renewed spiritual sense of God's love, I was on the right track. Nonetheless, my work was far from done. Coping skills like professional counseling and prescribed medication became a part of discovering freedom. One therapist encouraged me to take off the mask and not be afraid to show my true self. He said, "In my office, you don't have to be a wife, mom, or teacher; you can just be Shaneil "P.J." (my nickname, short for Precious Jewel) Yarbrough. My highest priority became self-love, which equaled the freedom to be my most authentic self. This transformation in thinking made it much easier to be consistently happy and resilient. Intentionally loving myself shaped my liberty. The lack of feeling loved has always been my motivation to be intentional about loving others. Whether members of my family (biological or adoptive), friends, colleagues, or people in general, I gladly put myself on the back burner deliberately to show I care. I hope people feel genuinely appreciated and special in my presence. One of the highest compliments my husband ever gave me is, "You taught me how to love people." He followed with what he has observed about me, "You are accepting, pass no judgment, and always kind." I intend always to be attentive, exchange kind words, and display gestures that go beyond the normal. I believe it is vital for people to feel comfortable being themselves. I want others to be better after coming in contact with me.

Interestingly enough, I give love as I do because of a few factors – my own experiences with disappointment, pain, and rejection. For too long, those three things influenced the absence of self-love. But, because of God's everlasting love for me, I eventually realized that I deserve love too, first from self. It took some time and practice before I actually knew what self-love looked like. Several years ago, during professional development training, an analogy I learned was doing what it takes to keep your cup full. The presenter reminded us that we can interact better with others when we first appreciate self (our strengths, experiences, and skills). Finding ways to "fill my cup" was a pivotal moment. And now that I have a full cup, I feel empowered and want to keep it that way. Reading God's word and how He feels about me was my first step. Then, I began reciting self-affirmations in the mirror and practicing those daily. Before long, I discovered many truths that helped to mold the liberty that I now enjoy.

Self- Love Truths

- ❖ I cannot change the situations I was born into (Born a Statistic), but I can choose my responses.

- ❖ What I have gone through does not have to determine where I am going.
- ❖ Time without talking will not heal my wounds.
- ❖ I can create an atmosphere conducive to my healing.
- ❖ Growing does not mean I've changed – it means I've allowed myself to become who God intended for me to be.
- ❖ I am responsible for my own happiness.

Because of these truths, I gradually found joy in being the light in my home. My husband might sum it up by saying, "Happy wife, happy life." It wasn't solely my husband's job to make sure I was happy. The responsibility I (and society) had put on my spouse was ultimately mine. The less I compared myself to others, worried about failing, and stopped seeking people's approval outside my home, the more I won my brightest freedom. For the sake of an example, I will share how I handled something simple, pre- and post-freedom. For over a decade, decorating for Christmas was a daunting task. When our sons were young, it was slightly more bearable, but I did it only for them. I reluctantly would drag the tree out two days before Christmas – just in time to place their gifts. Then, I quickly would put the tree back in the box and return it to storage. I allowed my unhappy memories of Christmas to minimize the joy of this time for my children. I once heard someone say, "If you don't get healed for yourself, do it for your children." I was a wounded parent but did not want to inflict the same wounds on our sons. I made the necessary adjustments within myself which ultimately blessed my children.

> **The less I compared myself to others, worried about failing, and stopped seeking people's approval outside my home, the more I won my brightest freedom.**

For the past three years, I haven't dreaded Christmas or the festive decorations. Like everything else in my life, I made plans to decorate. To my surprise, the simplistic designs that I came up with were enough to shock my husband and sons. Comments like, "Look at you going all out," "Wow, you're in the Christmas spirit," and "There's a little Christmas on the porch and several rooms!" prove that there is a significant difference. My reply to all their remarks was, "When you're free, you're free!" These actions will be the opposite of what you may have done (or not) before claiming freedom. For example, if you would usually walk down another aisle in the store when you see someone who hurt you, now, you would continue along your path without deviating from your initial plan. In the case of decorating and in many other ways, it was a win for our entire family. When freedom finally has been achieved, celebrating the success is crucial. Intentional moments of marking victories make it easier for progress to show up in other areas of our lives.

Career

Becoming more confident and consistently letting my light shine while at home worked to my career advantage. The techniques and strategies I used to be the best version of myself at home helped me flourish outside as well. When I heard of an opportunity to leave my work as a classroom teacher, it seemed exciting but terrifying. I mentioned the position to someone. She said, "You're young, you're a good teacher, and you should stay in the classroom." I valued her opinion but not her following comment. "They (referencing white administrators) will never give you that job." Those words posed a challenge.

Consequently, as in many times before, I found myself thinking, "I'll show them." My next conversation about the job was with a veteran teacher whom I considered a friend. Her insight as a black woman who had been a classroom teacher for a couple of decades was much different. She asked me whether I was qualified and whether I was interested in the new job. My answer to both questions was "yes." She followed with a critical statement, "Don't get stuck in the classroom like me. Use your gifts and talents – go for it! Her sentiments about being a good teacher but never going any further in her career stayed with me. I now realize she was encouraging me to let my light shine. With my husband also in my corner, I decided to pursue a new career path instead of running away.

The interview went well, and the transition to my new job was even smoother! I learned as much as possible, as quickly as possible. The role was new in the school district, which meant a lot of studying, meetings, note-taking, and asking questions. I was intrigued and willing to try new things as I was determined to succeed. I knew since I had taken the leap and accepted a new role, I had to commit wholeheartedly. My new work gave me the freedom to solve problems and think of unique solutions. The responsibilities of the position involved my exploring new thought processes and brought out my creative side. Our supervisor encouraged us to come up with ideas for supporting teachers and students. As the team and I developed plans and executed them in classrooms, everyone thrived.

It was during those two years that I began to excel in my career. I made the extra effort, upped my game, and took steps to fill in voids at the school. I showed up every day, took on extra duties, and stayed focused. I strived to be professional by following the rules. When dealing with my supervisor, co-workers, parents, and students, I was courteous, friendly, and tactful. I tried my best to express a positive attitude and always dressed appropriately. I could not afford to let anything adversely impact my advancement. As I took the initiative to discover better ways to get the job done and took constructive criticism gracefully, I accomplished even more.

The personal satisfaction I felt was motivation! I loved going to work. Being in good standing with my boss and colleagues was a bonus. This position's freedom allowed me to be myself, and it was a rare chance for a relatively new teacher to shine. Without this experience, I could have stumbled blindly into settling for the minimum. Thank goodness I didn't settle for less! Working in this role gave me a greater sense of trust in my abilities. I was in love with my new position and felt sure my career was on the right track. A "Help Wanted" ad in the local newspaper, presented by my husband, complicated my assurance. It wasn't long before I accepted another interview and was offered a position to work for a non-profit. If anyone had told me that I would be anything else, other than an elementary school teacher, I would have argued with them. I never imagined myself going beyond the classroom.

I thought I was living out my dream but soon realized my dream wasn't big enough. When our aspirations fit perfectly "in the box," we are more than likely stifling our potential. The Bible says God can do "immeasurably more than all we ask or imagine according to His power that is at work within us" (Ephesians 3:20). Tapping into what is inside us (the light of God) can propel us to new heights! The light illuminated during the time I spent at the non-profit. Even when I easily could have failed without the possibility of recovering, God was there. I am evidence that when God is for you, nothing can be against you! No enemy can separate us from Christ's love or dim our light. Racist remarks, jealousy, personal attacks, and many other weapons formed but did not prosper. The things that were meant to stop me and make me quit did the opposite! Knowing that God wants you to be free everywhere will change your perspective on life. You'll stop thinking of why you're not good enough, who isn't for you, when things will get better, and who doesn't like you. I had a lot of firsts during that work

> **I thought I was living out my dream but soon realized my dream wasn't big enough.**

experience. I supervised multiple individuals, facilitated professional development for a large group of people, and traveled out of state to present at a national conference.

I was in uncharted waters but discovered my God-given purpose! God's grace and favor took over before I knew it. Other agencies started noticing my strengths. Holding on to a good job is an accomplishment, so getting a job offer you weren't expecting is nothing short of a miracle! The more people I met, the more frequent invitations came for me to be a session presenter or keynote speaker. Opportunities started to fall in my lap unexpectedly. It wasn't until I began writing this book that I even considered making myself more marketable (and it still feels a little weird). While being pursued is nice, I always want to make sure it's a God-approved move. I have heard of the concept "too much, too soon." In my career, I desire to let my light shine. It is essential to me that the Supplier of that light be glorified above all things. This principle was initially easier at work than in my church and community-related experiences.

Church and Community

Sometimes I feel as though I am speeding through life. My first ministry, home, and a blossoming career keep me busy. I barely get a second of rest. As busy as I am, I always find time for both church and community work. The freedom that I have access to was first revealed at home and in my career. The liberation gives me a great sense of autonomy. But by no means do I consider myself to be an I-have-it-all-together person. I believe if such thoughts were even to come to mind, my affiliations in church and the community are sure to keep me grounded.

I found out some people have a problem being around other people who are okay with themselves. Confidence threatens people, especially religious or insecure people. Some view a person's self-assurance as a liability instead of inspiration. From the way I walk into a room, wear my hair, match my clothes, and even speak up, I can be mistaken as overbearing or a know-it-all. I am willing to tell the truth about who I really am, but others struggle to face the person behind their mask. My tendency to be transparent can also impede progress. No matter how much I showed up or made myself available to help, I was looked over and ignored. The phrase "know who you are and *whose* you are" is commonly used in the church. Yet, no one talks about what happens when individuals are fully aware of their identity in Christ. On the good days, I may feel invincible and on another as though I've done something wrong – all because of how others resist accepting me.

Honestly, I think it took the recognition I received in the early education field for some in the Christian community to see my value. Traditions, competition, and Satan's divisive traps to keep the church divided endangered my freedom to minister. Despite the internal changes I had experienced, initially, I was disconnected from using those ideas and strategies in a spiritual aspect. As believers, one of our most significant mandates is to share His goodness by increasing our capacity to love Him and others. This mandate doesn't mean we will preach a four-point sermon on a big stage. My first chances to be used by God certainly weren't. Radical change can take place in the intimate moments when ministering to a family member, a women's group at your local church, or to a friend. Meaningful conversations, lots of listening, and persistent prayers for real-life issues provide long-standing connections.

Through these connections, people can safely say, "We need to invite her to share with our group." Jesus was all about relationships. He developed intimacy and trust by doing life with the disciples. As they walked from place to place, I'm sure there was sharing of stories that included both weaknesses and strengths. This model builds comradery and ultimately produces changes in people. I achieve this comradery best when I reveal parts of myself. Authentically telling my story is not always easy, but it helps others see how similar we all are. Vulnerability broke the glass ceiling for me to be more freely welcomed in both the church and community. After Jesus was resurrected, He showed His scars with confidence and humility. Like Him, I want people to see my wounds as evidence of God's undeniable power. Satan wants us to think our imperfections are ugly and deforming. My Pastor (my husband) always says, "Never underestimate the power of your testimony – that is the best sermon anyone could ever preach."

> **Vulnerability broke the glass ceiling for me to be more freely welcomed in both the church and community.**

I use what God has brought me through to encourage others. Sharing my testimony has opened many doors. These engagements are in the church and in the community. I ran away from the title of "preacher" for many years because I was afraid that I would be viewed as trying to be something that I wasn't. I was perfectly fine with being "just P.J." In the black church, culturally, I am considered the "First Lady" as a Pastor's wife. When I was consecrated within our organization, I became a licensed "Evangelist Missionary." Later, I was charged as an "Ordained Minister." Regardless of the title, I want to spread the gospel of Jesus and serve His people. My hope rests humbly in who He has called me to be in all areas of my life.

Near the end of 2019, I had an itinerary for 2020 that literally made me scratch my head. Around that time, I honed in on re-centering myself to equip myself for what was ahead. I am by no means being braggadocios. Bear with me; I am trying to make a point. The following is a list of events that I had on my 2020 calendar (Prior to COVID-19):

> Christian Conferences (3 events)
> Early Childhood Conferences (3 events)
> Women's Day Celebrations (3 events)
> Youth-Related Events (2 events)
> Civic Events (3 events)

Fourteen unsolicited engagements were scheduled before the year began! When I look back on the old version of me, I was not only ill-equipped but also paralyzed by thoughts like "no one wants to hear what I have to say." Today, however, I affirm myself by saying, "I am redeemed – chosen by the Father who sees love and light when He looks at me." I would be seriously remiss if I did not freely serve His Kingdom and the community with my gifts and talents. Finally, I am most excited to share a part of my life where I am still working on fully unlocking the door of freedom – among my family and friends.

Family and Friends

I am not entirely comfortable writing this section. In fact, it took some time to decide whether I would. The first two times I sat down to record my thoughts, I experienced internal anxiety. Much as when I was writing my autobiography, I came to a speed bump that not only slowed me down but brought me to a screeching halt. As before, life began happening all around (close to the subject matter). I knew the danger of writing while in my emotions. I needed more time to pray and think. After I stepped away, I had a few things to consider. I contemplated, if I write this section, will my thoughts and stories dilute the concept of "L.I.F.E. after the Struggle?" While I have made substantial personal progress, at the same time, I am still working on being totally free in the presence of those closest to me.

John 4:44 says, "Now Jesus Himself had pointed out that a prophet has no honor in his own country." I can relate to this quote from the Bible. I am in no way calling myself Jesus or a prophet; however, I feel as though I am familiar with the rejection that He felt in his hometown (with family and friends). As they were with Him, people sometimes can be distracted by familiarity,

My experience is that I am not always accepted, because people knew me before God called me to these roles.

preconceived notions, and doubt. My day-to-day schedule is incredibly full, and I "wear many hats." In addition to my busy life of being a wife and mother, I am a pastor's wife, educator, ordained minister, author, motivational speaker, life coach, and community volunteer. My experience is that I am not always accepted, because people knew me before God called me to these roles. Even though I did not plan it (and sometimes wish it were not true), I have a publicly displayed life. One Pastor's wife described it as the "fishbowl" lifestyle. There is nowhere to hide. Almost weekly, people say hello or start conversations with me who think they know me. Long ago, I realized that my nickname makes me too easy to remember, yet, at the same time, I am seen as "P.J."– the family member, friend, or acquaintance they have always known.

I sincerely pray that I don't sound conceited or imply that I am somehow above others. At the same time, I want to share my heart's sentiments based on a few things I have encountered. I frequently find myself resisting the temptation to "shrink," ignore, or down-play what God is doing in my life. I would negate myself to avoid looking as if I am bragging. There is no doubt in my mind that His favor, grace, and anointing afford me each opportunity that comes my way! Hearing comments like, "Here comes the Super-Star…", "Make room for Mrs. Big Head!", and "You think you're something special, don't you?" make me feel uncomfortable. I am not exactly sure how I should respond or whether I should respond. Do I find a way to tone myself down or shift in some manner to match what others want? How do I avoid this unwanted attention? Sometimes a simple, "Stop it" or "Whatever" suffice, but other times I struggle with whether or not I am fully committed to knowing myself and being true to whom God has allowed me to blossom into. Being yourself takes courage and releasing the judgment of people. The first step towards fully being oneself is releasing judgment of self. Each day, I look in the mirror and speak positive words or recite positive affirmations about myself.

Learning the importance of radically accepting myself internally gives me the fortitude to ignore the external. This quick and simple practice has reduced the conscious and unconscious judgments that seemingly come from others.

Fulfilling my primary purpose, pleasing God, is what I most deeply care about. Bringing gladness to God involves getting out of my head, stepping away from the whirling thoughts, others' opinions, and being present in the moment. I either can waste time dealing with assumptions other people may have about me or come to terms with the fact that I never may have their approval. Besides, I am sure they have their own problems beneath their seeming confidence. What colossal relief it is to be a freer version of myself. Whether we feel deserving of this newfound prize or not, God puts us on display, much like a trophy of His grace. Because of God's grace, I am enough. I am smart enough, and I am important enough to be liked and accepted as I am. Humility must accompany truths like this. And we must never walk away from a chance to brag on God. He alone is worthy of honor, glory, and praise!

> **I either can waste time dealing with assumptions other people may have about me or come to terms with the fact that I never may have their approval.**

While I am bragging about God, I must pause to give Him credit for a few other things I have noticed about myself after the struggle. Only a few people have been brave enough to ask me if I have suffered any repercussions for sharing my life story candidly in my first book. Initially, my biggest reservation was that I would be accused of airing out dirty laundry or telling more than family and friends would be comfortable with. Now that I am on the other side of it, I would not change anything. There are no regrets. The shame, guilt, and pressure of hiding the truth were eating at me from the inside out. There were years of my life when I seemed okay. I was not. Simple gatherings, family events, and visits from different individuals would happen and literally zap my energy and send me into a wide range of negative emotions. For several days following these occurrences, I would be sad, withdrawn and find myself digging out of an emotional pit. It is so good to say, no longer! Case in point, in 2020, I experienced a first. At the age of 42, I ended the year with three instances of seeing my biological mother. I have never seen my mother that many times in the same calendar year. Furthermore, I never have handled the aftermath of being in her presence the way I was able to this year. Previously, I would be highly irritated and angry. Feelings attached to past occurrences robbed me of the present opportunity to be in the moment.

It may sound grim, but finally, I feel content in saying that I am at peace with our relationship. I have closure if I never see her again. I am sure that comment makes me sound like a nasty, dreadful person. My thoughts might give the impression that I am unforgiving or mean-spirited. But a cruel intention could not be farther away from the truth. Of course, I hope to have more time with her, and I continue to pray for her daily. It has taken me a long time to come to terms with my mother's lack of interest in a healthy and continuous relationship. Now I not only understand her but also understand my needs. Each of us has made choices for which we have to be accountable. Something likely happened to my mother that she has not resolved, and I am sorry for her unresolved pain. But it is not my responsibility to change or fix her. My responsibility is to love her. Loving someone does not mean we should allow his or her toxic behavior to affect us negatively. It can be a disturbing journey, but letting go of unrealistic expectations and taking responsibility for ourselves is a much better alternative.

I am healed. This healing did not come without intentionality as I worked hard and even re-entered therapy for a short season. I am grateful to be in a happy and healthy place. I could have chosen to spend the rest of my life struggling for something I may never get – my mother's unconditional love – but my choice is to live free. This decision has transcended every area of my life. Countless doors have opened for me confidently to put my true voice in the room (on various topics) as I have made this shift. And when we shift, we allow others the same opportunity. Family, friends, or foe, people no longer can hurt me, treat me any kind of way, and then I act as if I did something wrong.

I decide the outcome, and so can you. God gave me the strength to overcome what once was crippling. I have not mastered championing all aspects of life, but both large and small steps are progress. He did not need to hear why He should make things better for me. I didn't need to go down the list of how good I had been and how I did not deserve what I was going through. God does not need our resumes;

> **…people no longer can hurt me, treat me any kind of way, and then I act as if I did something wrong.**

He needs only our "Yes." "Yes, I trust You. "Yes, I need You above everyone else." "Yes, I will let my light shine even when life seems dark." This is an awakening that makes it possible to keep singing, "Everywhere I go, Everywhere I go, I'm gonna let it shine!"

L.I.F.E. *Affirmations*

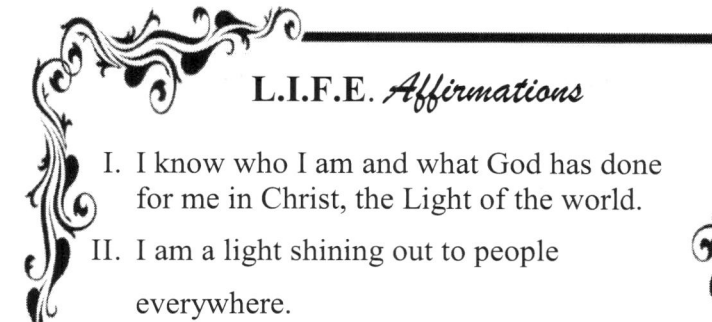

I. I know who I am and what God has done for me in Christ, the Light of the world.

II. I am a light shining out to people everywhere.

III. I will not hide or conceal my light.

CHAPTER 5
Live Freely and Love Deeply

Did you notice the title of the first four chapters? Read consecutively, they read, *A Life Worth Living After Finding Freedom Everywhere*. This phrase was planned as it outlines the title of the book. I hope I have adequately shared how to *Live in Freedom Everywhere (L.I.F.E.) after the Struggle*. You might consider this chapter a "bonus."

I wanted to convey explicitly that *Born a Statistic* was only the tip of the iceberg. Underneath the surface, there is always more! I can recall visiting my "Bigmama" (my grandmother) in Scott, Arkansas, as a girl. It was the late 80's, but she did not have running water in her modest country home. Outside in her yard was an old-school hand pump that was operated manually to pump water from the ground-installed well. As a child, I found it fun to pump water. There was something special about walking up to the pump on a scorching hot day, pumping the handle a few times, and having cool water come out into my cupped hand. Pumping water was exciting and different, but I did not understand the process of how it was possible. I noticed after about a minute of pumping, the water would begin to flow. From where was the water flowing?

In my study of the use of hand pumps for water wells, I learned the wells can be as deep as 273 inches (about 7 meters). I had no idea that water does not like to be pumped. The deeper the water is below the ground, the more reluctant it is to be drawn upwards. Sometimes, the water refuses to be pumped, which calls for specialized equipment. In the same fashion, when we want to go deeper in God, it takes a concentrated effort. Other words for an effort include energy, determination, work, and struggle. The success of our spiritual life will be reflected only in how deep we are willing to dig. If we dig only close to the surface when trouble and trials come, we will suffer. Lackluster efforts in our spiritual walk in prayer, Bible study, church attendance, and fellowshipping with like believers can lead to our finding ourselves grappling with the burdens of life. Those strains can be avoided. There is more under the surface when we are dedicated to cultivating our own spiritual growth as a daily practice. Developing our spiritual discipline is necessary to draw out the spiritual, living water (John 7:38), allowing us never to thirst again. Once we've put in the work, we are less likely to buckle under life's pressures. We can have a beautiful countenance in presence, words, and actions. To experience this achievement, I had to learn how to mitigate the stress of life and find a way to stay out of crisis mode. Escaping these critical moments required me to change the lens through which I had been viewing life and pushed me to go beyond my comfort zone. Although I grew up in a multi-generational environment, I did not witness my parents or grandparents articulating their struggles. Instead, I noticed their relationships with Christ without knowing the importance of making sure the connection was more than a surface-level encounter.

After I accepted Christ, within the confinements of religion, being a Christian became a mundane experience. Once the initial excitement wore off, I fell into complacency. Everything became routine: prayer time (check), mid-week Bible study (check), church on Sunday (check), give my tithe and offering (check), sing, lift my hands, and say amen (check), repeat (check). But I had drifted away from actively pursuing and loving God as Mark 12:30 says, "…love the Lord thy God

> **I had to learn how to mitigate the stress of life and find a way to stay out of crisis mode.**

with all thy heart, and with all thy soul, and with all thy mind, and with all thy strength: this is the first commandment." The pain of life once seemed tangible but was invisible. I had forgiven people but had not let go of the pain. I found myself in a love-hate relationship with pain. Without the Word of God to guide me, I never would have discovered a way to override the relentless pain. Reading about Joseph crying, Hannah wailing, and even Jesus asking, "My God, my God, why have You forsaken me" [Mark 15:34], gave me the approval needed. None of these Biblical characters kept his or her pain inside; each allowed himself or herself to feel it. A close friend once told me, "Surgery in the Kingdom does not have anesthesia or pain meds." Unfortunately, people cannot repay us for what they did, but they leave us holding the bag. We can complain, or we can create methods to move on – we cannot do both.

Nothing changes until behavior changes. We can't control people and outside events, but we can control our reactions and responses. For the sake of self-management, I have adopted an "excuse buster": Even though _____, how can I still _____? For example, "Even though *I feel the pain of what happened*, how can I *grow and learn from this experience*?"

Prayer, Praise, and Proclaiming

In a world full of negativity, it is vital to have a positive outlook on life. Almost like a magnet, we draw in what we think about. If we dwell on depressing, negative thoughts, we will be depressed and pessimistic. If we think positive, happy, and joyful thoughts, our lives will reflect and attract the same. If anyone wants to know one of my secrets, it's positivity. The Bible gives some instruction in achieving positivity in Philippians 4:8. It says, "Finally, brothers and sisters, whatever is true, whatever is noble, whatever is right, whatever is pure, whatever is lovely, whatever is admirable—if anything is excellent or praiseworthy—think about such things." Let's face it – that is sometimes easier said than done. Prayer, praising, and proclaiming His goodness are critical elements in remaining positive.

In *The Circle Maker: Praying Circles Around Your Biggest Dreams and Greatest Fears,* author Mark Batterson said, "Bold prayers honor God, and God honors bold prayers. God is not offended by your biggest dreams or boldest prayers. He is offended by anything less. If your prayers are not impossible to you, they are insulting to God." Challenges, adversity, hardships, and undesirable circumstances are no match for fervent prayer, because none of those can compare to God's ability! This realization gives me the confidence to pray simply but specifically. I love talking to God and pointing out His unique and unmatched characteristics. He inhabits (resides in) the praise of His people. The word "inhabits' does not mean God is present only when we praise Him. Thankfully, God is not confined to one place – He is omnipresent. But the composer of Psalm 22: 3 seems to imply that God is present and highly glorified when His name is lifted with honor. I believe God enjoys praise. I am well aware that He is deserving, and praise always draws me nearer to Him. As an attempt to capture God in a praiseworthy fashion, I asked my husband whether I could borrow one of his sermon conclusions, a favorite of mine. When he describes God (and His Son, Jesus) from A to Z, my husband (and Pastor) says the following:

> **If we think positive, happy, and joyful thoughts, our lives will reflect and attract the same.**

> He is my **A**ll-in-All, a **B**est Friend, He **C**ares, **D**eliverer, **E**verything, **F**aithful, **G**ood, **H**igh-Priest, **I**mmanuel, **J**ewel, **K**ing of Kings, **L**ord of Lords, **M**essiah, **N**ever leaves **N**or forsakes, **O**n-time, **P**rince of Peace, a **Q**uicker-picker-upper, **R**ighteous, **S**on of God, **T**rue Vine,

Understanding, **V**ictory, a **W**ay-out-of-no-way, **X**-tra, X-tra read all about Him, **Y**oke-destroyer, and He can make you **Z**estfully clean!

There is none like our God! Therefore, my prayers always begin with Him at the center. First, I thank Him for what He already has done, and then I approach His Spirit to guide me on how to pray. It has taken some time for me to relinquish the temptation to be in control. What He wants is what I want. Pursuing His priorities has become a way of life. Through consistent conversations with God, I have progressed a great deal. I have respect for His timetable, schedule, and ultimately, His will. When I pray, God always responds! Sometimes, it's a "Yes," other times it's a "No," and there are times He says, "Wait." Regardless of His response, I celebrate!

Any member of the Changing Lives Ministries Church family can answer this question: "What time is it?" The answer is, "CELEBRATION TIME!" At least monthly, I have the pleasure of posing this question to our congregation. This is a brief but notable time during our worship experience to praise and proclaim God's goodness! We all look forward to these moments as individuals, and their testimonies are recognized. Academic achievements, new jobs, sports highlights, debt cancellation, acquiring new homes, scholarships, and marriage engagements are among the things for which we collectively have praised God. I always am ready to join in on a praise party. I get most excited when I can hear every detail of how God made the impossible possible. He is faithful and has proven Himself time and time again! And I thoroughly enjoy proclaiming God's goodness! "Celebration Time" is one of my week's highlights. I love being a part of these uplifting and impactful displays of God's goodness. God is pleased when we recognize His name. As we tell others about what He has done, we acknowledge His power and love. Bragging on God moves Him to bless us even more. If you're like me, He has been so good that you wonder what you did to deserve these blessings? How is this my life? I still don't have the answers to those questions, but I will remain faithful to what I've been doing: praying, praising, and proclaiming His goodness!

> **As we tell others about what He has done, we acknowledge His power and love.**

Hope…Revealed

A gentleman I once encountered handed me a card from his wallet that read *H.O.P.E.: Having Only Positive Expectations*. The timing was perfect as I was feeling hopeless and was desperate for change. I know too well that "Hope deferred makes the heart sick…" (Proverbs 13:12). The absence of hope literally can make us sick – heartsick in our minds and souls. Walking in hopelessness is like entering the shallow end of a swimming pool. The longer you walk, the deeper it gets. After the water reaches your knees, you still can walk, but it's becoming more complex. Moving forward, as the water splashes against your shoulders and then ears, the water takes over, and you lose sight, sound, and breath. Flailing arms and kicking legs are no match for the rushing waters of hopelessness.

How can we find hope? Where can we look for it? How do we access the hope of Christ? As Christians, we learn that hope is unchanging and sure but sometimes forget to take advantage of it. On the darkest day in history, the work of Christ on the cross serves as a never-ending sign of hope. Hope is the assurance that something good is coming. Every day we have new mercies and new prospects to experience the hope of Christ. What He has available to us comes in abundance. It will not be just a little but heaping – running over! Don't be distracted by difficulties and trials. Hope has no limitations and will be revealed in due time. In Romans 8, Paul writes of this incredible hope in a way that inspired my personal ministry, Revealed Ministries!

Romans 8:18 is the foundational scripture of this ministry: "For I consider that the sufferings of this present time are not worthy to be compared with the glory which shall be REVEALED in us." Time is explored in Ecclesiastes 3 and indicates a time for every matter and every work (3:17). We cannot escape the trouble, because God uses all of it to perfect our character. A diamond looks like an ordinary rock in the rough, but after it is cut, beauty emerges. As the stone goes through the finishing process, the diamond craftsman holds it up against a large grinding wheel. The process takes a long time, depending on the quality desired. This is the way God works on us. It is not always pleasant, but the Divine Craftsman gets the final glory when we are finished. Suffering indeed reveals favorable results. God is glorified, believers purified, and the lost justified.

> A gem cannot be polished without friction,
> nor a man perfected without adversity.
> – Seneca The Younger

Maximized Motivation

I dedicated my first book to my husband and two sons. Their unwavering love and support were my motivation to achieve the long-time dream of becoming an author. Once it was released at my 40th birthday party, I was relieved but also challenged. It became apparent to me that as people began to read, I would be held accountable. I had very little concern about what I shared, because it was not only "my truth," it was "the truth." However, I was also aware that my words would demonstrate how my sons and others could overcome anything. Not too long ago, I was asked to make a list of places, events, and conferences where I had served as the motivational speaker or deliver the keynote address. I also have been asked numerous times how I ended up on the speaker's circuit.

Viewing my thirteen-year-long list of public speaking presentations goes beyond my wildest expectations. Full disclosure – it happened by accident. When I started giving these talks in the early childhood community and in ministry, I had the same goals: to do it for the right reasons and to be effective. Career-wise, I wanted to be credible and creative. In ministry, I tried to be relevant and real. And in all cases, I desire to help others be better. *Mr. Rogers' Neighborhood,* one of my favorite childhood television shows, featured Mr.

Fred Rogers, who was a master of this concept. He once said, "When I was a boy, and I would see scary things in the news, my mother would say to me, 'Look for the helpers. You will always find people who are helping.'" I take great joy in being a helper.

I want to show people (beginning with my children, family, and loved ones) that I have done the work. I want to be viewed as someone who goes above and beyond, can be trusted by others, and chases what seems impossible. I no longer want only to look as though I have my life together. I wish genuinely and exceptionally to be satisfied with my life. My prayer is that my everyday life is a demonstration of motivation. It is important to be liked and sometimes entertain an audience, but authenticity is key. I know firsthand that life can be achingly difficult. I am confident that each of my disappointments has been necessary. If they were not, God would not have allowed them. I hope to spread the message that one day we all will see how He used our pain and losses to accomplish far more than we ever imagined. I pray that you are motivated amid your struggle. As the saying goes, "Life is tough, but so are you." With the help of our Father, you are stronger than the struggle!

My Mantra

In nearly every book I ever have autographed, I have added the inscription, "Live Freely and Love Deeply." When I share a video on social media, I usually sign off with those words. These are the things I remind myself to do each day. They have become my mantra. One definition of a personal mantra is a positive phrase or affirmative statement for the purpose of motivation or encouragement. A mantra can be a quote, power phrase, scripture, or anything that resonates with you. One day I was talking to someone about how

I no longer want only to look as though I have my life together. I wish genuinely and exceptionally to be satisfied with my life.

empowering it is to share about my life. I told her that I am evidence that with God, we can "Live Freely and Love Deeply." I don't know how my mind put these words together, but I recall the first time I felt they finally applied to my life.

Live Freely

Ephesians, chapter one, gives a list of many good things that are true for those of us, including me, who will accept them. The list includes:

> Adopted
> Blessed
> Chosen
> Free

After many years of not experiencing these realities, I realized I had not truly accepted them. Finally, I am at a point in my life where I want to acquire all that God has for me. I have embraced the spirit of living freely. A word to the wise, to "Live Freely," can be a little funny. I think we all want it but do not always make the necessary changes to get it. Though many of us are not behind bars, we have experienced being bound by life. Constant worries and stress can lead to our being overburdened. When we focus on the past, it is difficult to enjoy the present, and it becomes impossible to see the future. However, I realize the only thing I possess is in the present. Therefore, I cherish the present moment and make the best of it. I have let go of what is behind me to experience fully each moment – freely.

What people see externally in me is not as important as my intrinsic desire to be my best self and succeed. I try to observe adversities and mistakes as chances to learn. I am less judgmental of myself, and I don't compare myself to others.

I strive to walk in humility, and I am willing to admit I am wrong and apologize. I look forward to feedback from others and use it to take steps in the right direction. I am surrounded by trustworthy, positive, and supportive people who encourage me to walk in my freedom. They continue to bring out the best in me. As a life-long learner, I always am watching and searching for new, more efficient ways to grow as a person. I strive to do this process of improving with no pressure, because I know surrendering to God releases even more freedom.

Those who know me know that I am known for keeping a strict schedule and like to see every detail of each day. But sometimes, I put too much emphasis on making plans and strategies. In the end, God is in control, and I embrace that fact, realizing if I don't check all of the boxes, He will. In this place of freedom, things are never bad. They may be challenging, interesting, or different. But because I am living freely, I accept what is and what will be.

Love Deeply

For much of my life, I was very cautious, almost afraid of love. That's because love has, many times, made me feel pain. The word itself is easy to say but more difficult actually to do.

Some people use it very loosely, and it becomes a superficial word they say with little to no thought. With age and maturity, I am careful not to throw the word around lightly. And when I hear people that do, I cringe at the thought of love being devalued. Put simply, I believe love is more than just a word.

Love is an action and feeling – a verb if you will. The four-letter word itself doesn't hold much weight, but the unlimited amount of emotion that can accompany it can be deep. Love is powerful. It can shield you from pain, protect, nourish, and make you whole. I have pondered love a lot, because God is love. Andrae' Crouch composed a song that goes,

> I don't know why Jesus loved me.
> I don't know why He cared.
> I don't know why He sacrificed His life.
> Oh, but I'm glad, so glad He did.

Each time I sing those lyrics, they resonate in my heart, mind, and soul. No one's love can compare to the depth of His love. This depth is based on the cost that He paid.

God made the ultimate sacrifice for us, which assures us of a more profound love than we are capable of matching. When I think of how little we deserved this love, I am in awe. I have not treated Him well all my life and have not done all that He expects, but He loves me. I have offended Him and shunned Him, yet His love deepens. This example of love provides us with what we need to fulfill the greatest commandment (love God) and the second greatest commandment (love your neighbor). We have to satisfy these instructions because they are essential to God. And if we love God most, we will love others to the best of our ability. I am a work in progress, and I don't always love as well as I should.

> **The four-letter word itself [love] doesn't hold much weight, but the unlimited amount of emotion that can accompany it can be deep.**

Admittedly, I do not like some people. That phrase may sound harsh, so I will soften it by saying some people are hard to like. Maybe I should I say I don't like their ways of being. I'm not naïve – some people don't like me either. I guess that's life. Consequently, nothing bothers me more than innocent people being hurt, wronged, and treated poorly. Maybe I am for the "underdog" because I often have been one myself. Liking and loving are similar but clearly different in so many ways. Along my Christian journey, I have learned to love those whom I don't like. I am concerned about them, pray for them, and ask God to bless them. And I know only

He can change them. I believe if I continue in faith and love, God will deal with them, just as He deals with me. When I strive [through the Holy Spirit] to see them as God sees them, I can love them as He does. I know I have been unlikeable, yet God loves me still. I once read, "You will never look into the eyes of someone who God does not love." Of course, we won't always find it easy to love everyone, but God can help us be kind, respectful, and fair.

I am thankful that I've made so much progress. But progress does not mean perfection. In my human nature, I want to reserve my love for those who will reciprocate it. Therefore, I had to come to terms that the absence of an apology doesn't mean nothing happened. But we cannot expect an apology from someone who doesn't have the capacity (and/or desire) to offer one. Our pain and disappointment are deserving of kindness. We have to accept the things we cannot change and love ourselves enough to begin an independent healing process. Through love for myself, I learned that healing (spiritual, mental, or emotional) was for me – not others. Some people don't have the capacity for the improved, loving version of me. I don't get upset when they say, "You've changed," because as a matter of fact, I have...for the better! To love deeply means to love God, love others, and love yourself.

L.I.F.E. *Affirmations*

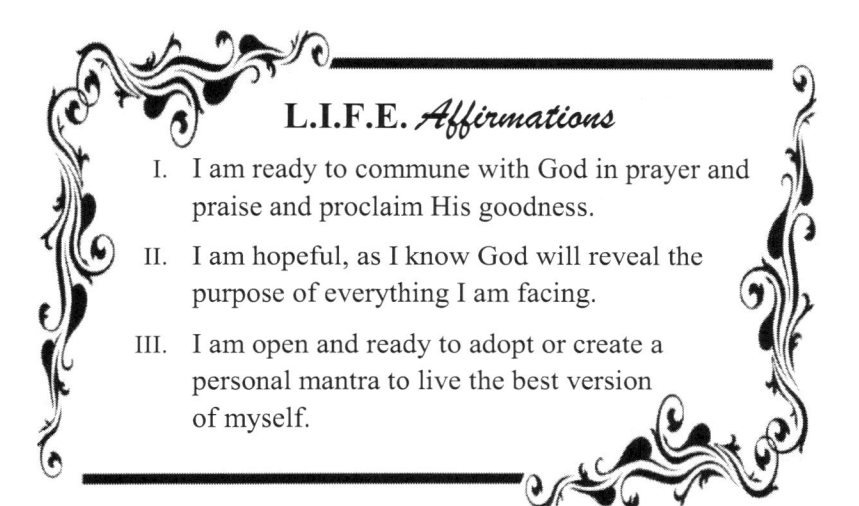

I. I am ready to commune with God in prayer and praise and proclaim His goodness.

II. I am hopeful, as I know God will reveal the purpose of everything I am facing.

III. I am open and ready to adopt or create a personal mantra to live the best version of myself.

Disclaimer:

Shaneil "P.J." Yarbrough is not, nor does she claim to be a medical professional. If you are having thoughts of harming yourself or dealing with a life crisis, please contact a skilled, trained professional.

Share Your Thoughts

Would you like to share your thoughts with the author? She loves any opportunity to personally connect with readers. Your feedback and comments will be forwarded when you visit www.ShaneilPJYarbrough.com or email SYRevealedMinistries@yahoo.com. Also, please submit your review of this book on Amazon. Thank you for your support!

Notes and References

[1] Gaither Music TV (2020, April 12). *Because He Lives (with Bill Gaither Introduction) – Gaither Vocal Band [Live]* [Video]. Retrieved November 25, 2020. https://www.youtube.com/watch?v=paXNlvy-hq8

[2] oChristian.com (2019). Paul Chappell Quotes. Retrieved November 28, 2020 from http://christian-quotes.ochristian.com/Paul-Chappell-Quotes/

[3] Life Application Study Bible, New Living Translation, explanatory footnotes (Genesis 48 verses 1-45) – 2015; Tyndale House Foundation Publishers, Inc. Carol Stream, Illinois 60188

[4] Innocence Project (2020, December 29). About. Retrieved from https://innocenceproject.org/about/

[5] https://www.pbs.org/wgbh/americanexperience/features/freedomsummer-hamer/

Made in the USA
Columbia, SC
30 August 2021